the MISO BOOK

the Art of Cooking with Miso

john & jan BELLEME

SQUAREONE
PUBLISHERS

COVER DESIGNER: Phaedra Mastrocola
COVER PHOTO: Getty Images, Inc.; and John Belleme
INTERIOR PHOTOS: John Belleme
INTERIOR ART: Kathe Cobb
IN-HOUSE EDITOR: Marie Caratozzolo
TYPESETTER: Gary A. Rosenberg

Square One Publishers
115 Herricks Road
Garden City Park, NY 11040
(516) 535-2010 • (877) 900-BOOK
www.squareonepublishers.com

Library of Congress Cataloging-in-Publication Data

Belleme, John.
  The miso book : the art of cooking with miso / John Belleme, Jan Belleme.
    p. cm.
Includes index.
ISBN 0-7570-0028-2 (pbk.)
  1. Cookery (Miso) 2. Miso. I. Belleme, Jan. II. Title.
TX819.M57B45 2004
    641.6'5655—dc22

                                                    2004004180

Printed in the United States of America

10 9 8 7 6 5 4 3 2 1

Contents

To John Jr., Justin, and Michael
with our gratitude and love.

Acknowledgments

This book would not have been written or even imagined without the efforts of hundreds of natural foods pioneers who sparked the interest and markets for miso and other natural foods. We are particularly indebted to the early Zen and macrobiotic movements, which created the opportunity for companies such as Erewhon, Eden, Westbrae, Tree of Life, Great Eastern Sun, Granum, Clearspring, and Natural Import Company to begin importing large shipments of miso and other traditional Japanese foods. Without the great efforts of these companies and people, miso would never have become as popular and well-known as it has.

We want to acknowledge the significant influence that *The Book of Miso* by Bill Shurtleff and Akiko Aoyogi had on the popularity of miso in the West. Their books about miso and other Japanese foods have been an inspiration to us.

We would especially like to thank Takamichi and Itsuko Onozaki and their family for sharing their home and centuries-old knowledge of Japanese miso craftsmanship with foreigners who could hardly speak a word of their language. Their adventurous yet traditional spirit, as well as their example and teaching has had a profound impact on our lives since we met in 1979. We also want to thank Akiyoshi Kazama, founder and president of Mitoku

Company in Tokyo, who accomplished the almost impossible task of helping us find the Onozaki family.

This book would not have been written if it were not for our opportunity to be part of the conception, founding, and building of the American Miso Company. Natural foods businessman Sandy Pukel of Miami, Florida, had the original idea of making miso in the United States. We are grateful for the profound influence he has had on our lives. We also want to give special thanks and appreciation to Barry Evans, who has been successful in keeping American Miso going for over twenty years. We would like to thank the miso makers who came after us, particularly Don Debona and Greg Gonzales.

Mitoku Company and its staff and suppliers provided some of the information we have gathered for this book. We are particularly indebted to Christopher Dawson, who is now the CEO of Clearspring, in London, and who spent many years at Mitoku. Christopher gave us a great deal of information on the history and craft of making traditional Japanese foods. We are also very grateful to Tomoko Katagiri, of Mitoku, who has translated Japanese texts and contacted Japanese miso experts on our behalf. Kaoru Theado also deserves thanks for her skillful translations of Japanese texts. Leila Bakkum, who can type faster than we can think, gets a special thanks for saving us hours of typing.

Finding new and stimulating ways to use miso that are both simple and flavorful is a challenge. For help, particularly in the soup and fish chapters, we turned to award-winning chef John Belleme, Jr. John is a graduate of the Culinary Institute of America, co-founder of Zemi restaurant in Boca Raton, Florida, and a region-ally acclaimed chef who has a flair for blending Asian and Western ingredients to create delicious foods with unique flavors.

Finally, we would like to thank all those on the staff of Square One Publishers, especially publisher Rudy Shur for his guidance and vision, and Marie Caratozzolo, our editor, for her patience, encouragement, and editorial expertise.

Introduction

The world's most ancient cultivated plants were not grains and vegetables but rather microscopic organisms—molds, yeast, and bacteria—that cause foods to ferment. Our ancestors stumbled upon the fermentation process, probably quite by accident, when they discovered that adding the right amount of salt to food prevented it from spoiling. The salt also transformed the molecular structure of the food, making it more flavorful and digestible. Through the magic of fermentation, we have learned to harness the microbial world to do our "fireless cooking," transforming such foods as cabbage into sauerkraut, cucumbers into pickles, and milk into yogurt and cheeses. In Japan, through a centuries-old double-fermentation process, soybeans and grains are transformed into miso—one of the country's most revered culinary treasures.

For the Japanese, miso preparation is considered an art form, and those who prepare it are considered Masters. As a food, miso is used to flavor and enhance the nutritional value of a wide variety of savory and satisfying dishes. As a folk remedy, it has been successfully used to treat digestive problems, cancer, radiation sickness, tobacco poisoning, and even low libido—to the point that its healing properties have been confirmed by modern science. With varieties that offer an incredible diversity of colors,

tastes, and textures, miso is no longer a secret of Eastern cuisine. This Japanese fermented food is slowly expanding its reach, stimulating the creativity of cooks around the world.

Japan is a densely populated island with scant natural resources. During preindustrial times, the very survival of the Japanese people may well have depended on the development of their unique and diversified fermentation processes. In fact, Japan's two most important foods, rice and soybeans, have been preserved for centuries through the miso-making process. Before the advent of refrigeration and food preservatives, miso was the country's emergency ration of choice, and every family had a keg stored away for hard times. Indeed, with its essential vitamins and minerals and excellent balance of carbohydrates, fats, and proteins, miso is one of nature's perfect survival foods. Properly stored, miso can provide life-sustaining nourishment decades after it is made.

Until modern times, most Japanese families started their day with a bowl of miso soup (many still do). In fact, it is not unusual for families living in the countryside, where there are fewer food choices, to have miso several times a day. According to our miso teacher, Takamichi Onozaki, as recently as the 1960s, it was common for rural families to make their own miso or buy unfermented (raw) miso from the local miso maker to ferment in their homes. Each family took pride in fermenting its own miso, and the subtle difference between various homemade varieties was often the subject of endless conversation. This preference for "home brews" extended beyond the home to include hundreds of local variations, which represented the different regions and climates of the Japanese islands. Names such as Tsugaru, Kaga, Gozen, Sanuki, Fuchu, and Setouchi are just a few of the hundreds of local and regional varieties of miso, each with its own characteristic flavor, texture, and color.

The Miso Book includes everything you will ever want to know about this healthy, delicious, and versatile food. Part One, appropriately titled "All About Miso," includes three informative chapters on various aspects of miso. Chapter 1, "Shedding Light on Miso," presents some miso basics—how it is made, the ingredients used, and the various types. It also offers helpful tips on how to determine product quality before making a miso purchase. Chapter 2, "Miso Medicine," offers a comprehensive report on miso's incredible health benefits, which are supported by the scientific research of several countries (as well as traditional Japanese folklore). Little-known facts about miso's extraordinary healing power will amaze and inspire you to include this food in your daily diet. Chapter 3 guides you in "Making Miso at Home." Before the Second World War, it was common for the Japanese people to make their own miso, using generations-old family recipes. This chapter offers clear, easy-to-follow instructions to help you start your own family tradition of putting up miso.

Rounding out Part One are two fascinating insets on the production of this Japanese main-stay. In "The Miso Master's Apprentice," you'll hear the true story of the apprenticeship we served under miso master Takamichi Onozaki. It was in his small family-run shop in rural Japan that we learned the ancient craft of miso making—an experience that changed our lives forever. "Breakfast of Emperors" takes a look at one of Japan's oldest and most prestigious miso factories. More than a business, the Hatcho Miso Company is a Japanese institution; one that has also has played an important role in Japan's military history.

Part Two of The Miso Book begins with a chapter that details everything you'll need to know when cooking with this exceptional food. It includes general guidelines as well as specific tips for using miso to create dishes that are both healthful and delicious. The balance of chapters in Part Two offers over 140 easy-to-follow recipes that include miso in a wide variety of appetizers, entrées, and everything in between. You'll find flavorful salad dressings, satisfying soups, delicious sauces, sensational seafood dishes, and much, much more. Many of these recipes are traditional family favorites, some are new creations, and others are adaptations of dishes we've enjoyed at fine restaurants. Best of all, the recipes are easy to prepare—even the novice cook will find success.

Miso is a super food; by simply having a bowl of miso soup each day, you can begin to experience its health benefits. But if you want to enjoy miso's full culinary potential, incorporate it a number of dishes, beginning with the choices offered in this book. With miso as a part of your diet, you'll soon discover for yourself why it is considered such a dietary asset in the Japanese cuisine.

All
About
Miso

1. Shedding Light on Miso

Miso, a fermented soy product, is one of the world's most delicious, versatile, and medicinal foods. An ancient Far Eastern staple, miso began appearing on natural food store shelves in the West in the 1970s and has since established itself as an essential ingredient in the natural food cuisine.

It's no wonder that miso is growing in popularity among health-conscious Americans. In addition to offering great flavor and versatility in recipes, miso is credited with numerous health benefits, including lowered cholesterol, chronic pain reduction, alkalinized blood, lowered blood pressure, and the reduced risk of some forms of cancer. Its daily use is also responsible for canceling the harmful effects of certain carcinogens. (See Chapter 2 for more details on miso's health benefits). Furthermore, unpasteurized miso is abundant in beneficial microorganisms and enzymes that aid digestion, reduce food allergies, destroy pathogenic bacteria and toxins, and aid in food assimilation. Miso is simple to incorporate into dishes and can enhance every course from hors d'oeuvres and salads to entrées and desserts. It works well in basic macrobiotic fare as well as gourmet creations.

This chapter presents some miso basics. It includes information on the ingredients commonly used to make miso, the various miso types, and the different manufacturing methods. It also discusses freeze-drying as an effective preservation method.

WHAT IS MISO?

Miso is a fermented soy food that may have originated in China around 800 BC and later spread, along with Buddhism, to the island of Japan about 500 AD. Considered a super food by some natural healers, it is usually made from cooked soybeans and cultured grains such as rice or barley.

Once the soybeans have been cleaned and cooked, they are mixed with koji (grain inoculated with *Aspergillus* culture), salt, and water. This mixture is then left to ferment. Gradually, the enzymes supplied by the koji along with microorganisms from the environment break down the complex structure of the beans and grains into readily digestible amino acids, fatty acids, and simple sugars. The result is a concentrated purée that adds both flavor and healthful benefits to food.

MAKING MISO

Miso is such a unique and vital food, it is important to clearly understand the factors that influence its taste, medicinal qualities, and nutritional value. By far, the most important of these influences are manufacturing methods and quality of ingredients. Basically, there are three methods of miso manufacturing. In order of decreasing quality, they are: traditionally made, naturally aged, and temperature-controlled. Although these methods differ, depending on the type of miso being made and the level of technology employed, the basic process dates back to preindustrial Japan.

Traditionally Made

Currently, less than 5 percent of Japanese miso is traditionally made. In the relatively few shops that still use traditional methods, making miso is a way of life (see "The Miso Master's Apprentice" beginning on page 9). Each family member from grandchild to grandmother has important responsibilities each day that center around the miso-making process. The hallmark of this traditional procedure is the handmade koji, which is made in an unheated koji room. In this uniquely constructed area, the heat and humidity that are naturally generated by the fermenting grain are carefully monitored for forty-eight hours until the mature koji, covered with a fluffy, white, glistening mycelium, is sweet and loaded with powerful digestive enzymes.

Making koji this way is a labor-intensive process that requires skill, sensitivity, and stamina. In large shops that make up to 2,000 pounds of koji at once, workers spend almost all day in the koji room where the oxygen is low, the temperature is very high, and the humidity is 100 percent. One of our Japanese helpers at American Miso Company lost four pounds in one day while working in the koji room!

In preindustrial Japan, the koji room was the domain of the miso master, and slight local variations in the process were closely guarded secrets. The few remaining Japanese miso masters believe traditional miso's characteristic

heightened medicinal value and deep rich flavor result from the following:

❏ High-quality ingredients, such as organic grains and beans, sun-dried sea salt, and pure natural water.

❏ Strong koji that effectively breaks down the beans and grains.

❏ Slow cooking and cooling of soybeans.

❏ Long established strains of "wild" microorganisms that permeate the developing miso.

❏ Unhurried natural aging in old, seasoned wooden vats.

Whenever possible, traditionally made miso is the type to choose. It is usually sold unpasteurized and must be kept refrigerated.

Naturally Aged

Although traditionally made miso is always "naturally aged," these two words can also refer to mass-produced miso that is fermented at natural temperatures, often in stainless steel or plastic tanks. In this type of naturally aged miso, the koji process is usually completely automated, and every effort is made to keep wild organisms out of the miso.

Soybeans are rapidly cooked and cooled, while koji is automatically made in large stainless steel rooms using warm, humid, purified air. To reduce cost and the need for experienced workers, hand labor is minimal. The quality of ingredients in this type of miso varies with market objectives. A few manufacturers make organic varieties. The finished product has a uniform taste, color, and texture, and is usually sold pasteurized in sealed plastic bags that need no refrigeration. This is the type of miso that is commonly sold in American natural foods markets.

Temperature Controlled

The lowest quality miso is the temperature-controlled commercial variety. Through a rapid, high-tech, high-temperature process, red miso can be made in only one to two months—a far cry from the one to two years it takes to ferment naturally. To insure the quality of fermentation and to accelerate the process, traditional and natural miso makers customarily use "seed" miso from a previous batch as an inoculum. Commercial miso makers, on the other hand, accelerate fermentation by adding concentrated starters that contain yeast and lactic acid bacteria before incubation. With the addition of heat and starters, sweet miso, which naturally ferments in about one to two months, can be made in just a few days! Miso that is made through a temperature-controlled process has a flat, sometimes burnt taste.

After World War II, almost all large Japanese factories converted to the temperature-controlled incubation method, which now accounts for most Japanese miso. Although this type of miso is usually sold pasteurized or with chemical preservatives, some American natural foods stores and Asian markets sell unpasteurized varieties.

TYPES OF MISO

In Japan there are as many types of miso as there are different varieties of cheese sold in the United States. Varying the kinds of grain used, the ratio of grains to beans, the salt content, and the length of fermentation all play a role in miso's diversity. However, for practical purposes, miso can be divided into two large groups based on color and taste.

Sweet miso is usually light in color (white, yellow, or beige) and high in carbohydrates. It is marketed under such names as "mellow miso," "sweet miso," and "sweet white (*shiro*) miso." Because it is high in koji and low in salt and soybeans, sweet miso naturally ferments in just two to eight weeks, depending on the exact recipe and the temperature during the aging process.

Miso with a higher salt content, lower koji content, and proportionally more soybeans is darker in color and saltier in taste than sweet miso. It must be fermented for a longer period of time, usually at least one summer, but as long as two to three years in extremely cold climates. This type of miso is marketed under such names as "red (*aka*) miso," "rice (*kome*) miso," "brown rice (*genmai*) miso," and "barley (*mugi*) miso." Soybean misos such as *mame* and *hatcho* are also dark, salty varieties.

Determining Quality

When considering quality, some miso advocates insist on using dark miso that has been aged for at least two years. Although there is scientific evidence that suggests dark, long-aged miso is much more effective than sweet miso in the treatment of some forms of cancer, high cholesterol, and radiation sickness, there is also evidence that sweeter, lighter miso has its own medicinal benefits. It is amazing to many Japanese people that some Americans are willing to pay more for miso that is over-aged for several years and almost black in color. In fact, miso that is aged too long, regardless of the type, deteriorates in taste, color, aroma, enzymatic activity, and nutritional value.

It is important to understand that each miso is made from its own recipe, and each recipe has a proper aging time. Light, sweet miso is not merely dark, salty miso that has fermented for less time. Red miso, in the early stages of fermentation, is light in color, but very salty and raw tasting. Sweet, light miso that is fermented for too long will turn dark and lose its fresh, sweet taste. In a few months, it will look somewhat like two-year red miso. The point here is simple: what actually determines the color, taste, and overall quality of miso is not long aging but proper aging. Proper aging is determined by the specific recipe and climate.

In the cool areas of northern Japan, natural, high-quality miso is aged for two years, while in areas like Fukuoka, which is hot and humid, it is aged for only two months. Between these two extremes are hundreds of age-old regional miso recipes. Of course, local residents all claim that their miso is the best.

While living in Japan, we were surprised to learn that what actually determines which type of miso is popular in any particular area depends just as much on the historical availability of grains and soybeans and economics as it does on local tastes. For example, in parts of Japan where rice is plentiful, rice misos are popular; in the mountainous regions where barley is grown, barley miso is the variety of choice. This is also true of soybean misos, which are popular in Japan's central region where soybeans are plentiful. The cost of grains also influences Japan's traditional taste for miso. In the less affluent, rural mountain areas, barley miso is often the only kind available. By contrast, in the wealthier urban areas around Tokyo and Kyoto, many types of rice miso, particularly sweet rice misos, dominate. In fact, even today in Japan's metropolitan areas, barley is considered a poor man's miso. Speaking very generally, dark, salty misos seem to be preferred by the more physically active rural population, while sweet, light varieties are the choice among city dwellers.

When Used in Cooking

Each type of miso has its own use in terms of both health maintenance and cooking. While dark miso is excellent for hearty winter cooking, sweet miso is great in summer soups, dips, sauces, and salad dressings. (See "Cooking Guidelines," beginning on page 39.)

In terms of health or food value, light, sweet miso is high in simple sugars and contains more lactic acid bacteria and about twice as much niacin than dark, salty varieties. Dark miso is higher in protein and, because of its greater proportion of soybeans, contains more saponin, lecithin, fatty acids, and isoflavones—all of which have important health benefits.

It is not always possible to determine the type of miso you are choosing from the name printed on the label. For example, although names such as "brown rice miso" and "barley miso" usually refer to products that are fermented for a year or more, this is not always the case. However, information on the label can help you determine if the miso is long-aged. FDA regulations require that manufacturers list the ingredients on their labels in descending order by weight. When shopping for long-aged miso, check the ingredients. If soybeans appear on the ingredient list before rice or barley, you can be sure you are buying long-aged miso.

However, do not let your concern with miso's medicinal properties eclipse your culinary enjoyment of this truly delicious food. When choosing miso, look for organic, traditionally made, unpasteurized miso, and then let your personal needs and taste be your guide.

PRESERVING MISO

As a method of preserving miso, freeze-drying is ideal. Under the right conditions, water molecules in foods can change directly into a gas without first passing through a liquid phase. This dehydration process, called *sublimation*, involves freezing food under a vacuum, which allows the water to vaporize at a very low temperature. Freeze-dried miso retains an excellent flavor profile, because very little of the fresh taste is lost during this process. Moreover, this type of drying removes water molecules from bioactive compounds without destroying their chemical integrity. Theoretically, along with the microorganisms, most of the medicinal components of miso, such as essential fatty acids, melanoidins, saponins, isoflavones, and lecithin, are also preserved.

Because astronauts eat freeze-dried foods during space travel, freeze-dried miso, which is available in instant soups and ramen broths, is often marketed as a "space-age food." Interestingly, although we may consider freeze-drying as "space age," the Japanese have been making snow-dried tofu for hundreds of years. Freeze-dried foods were also a staple of the Peruvian Incas, who preserved vegetables using this technique high in the Andes. However, ancient freeze-drying is a much better way of preserving miso and other fermented foods than simple heat dehydration, which works fine for fruits and vegetables, but greatly reduces the quality of delicate fermented foods. When shopping for dehydrated miso products, look for the words "freeze-dried" on the package.

THE POPULARITY GROWS

Miso's popularity in the West continues to increase as more and more people discover its extraordinary health benefits and culinary possibilities. In addition to finding miso on store shelves, expect to see this vital soy food added to many prepared commercial foods, such as salad dressings, dips and spreads, as well as instant foods that include freeze-dried miso.

The Miso Master's Apprentice
Making Miso in a Traditional Shop

Hoping to learn the art of making traditional miso, in the fall of 1979, we set out to find a miso master with a big heart and a willingness to teach. With the help of Akiyoshi Kazama, president of Mitoku Company, we found such a man—Takamichi Onozaki. From his family shop located in a small village in rural Japan, Onozaki produced over 100 tons of organic barley and brown rice miso each year. This was a sizable amount, considering the simplicity of his equipment and size of his labor force. Our eight-month stay with the Onozaki family had a profound, positive influence on our lifestyle, health, and appreciation for traditional Japanese food and culture.

The first few weeks in our new surroundings were overwhelming—a cultural vertigo. However, Mr. Onozaki's faith and patience, combined with our driving passion to learn his craft, helped ease our transition into this unfamiliar new world.

The Onozakis made traditional miso; traditional in the sense that their basic production methods have been the same for generations. Although they had purchased some simple equipment to accommodate the ever-increasing demand for their product, the family's methods for making *koji* (cultured grain used as a starter) and fermenting the miso were the same as those used by their ancestors.

Although we knew that our apprenticeship would involve hard work and sacrifice, it was much more intense than we had anticipated. The hours were long and exhausting, and our bodies were often exposed to temperatures of extreme hot and cold. At first, it felt as if we were being stretched beyond our limits of endurance. Taking inventory of sore body parts became a morning ritual. But within a few weeks, the Onozaki lifestyle—living under natural conditions with little heat and strong food—soon provided us with the strength and stamina we needed to continue.

Each weekly miso-making cycle was almost exactly the same. First, the koji was made; then the soybeans were prepared. At the end of the week, the beans were mixed with koji, salt, and water to start the fermentation process.

On the first day of the cycle, approximately 1,500 pounds of pearled barley or lightly milled rice were washed and then left to soak overnight. In the morning, the grain was steamed, and then allowed to cool until it was just warm to the touch. Next, *Aspergillus oryzae* spores, called *tane koji,* were hand rubbed into the warm grain. Once inoculated, the grain was transferred to a long crib that was set in the middle of the koji room—a dark place with thick walls and a dirt floor. After being covered with four or five blankets, the inoculated grain was left to incubate overnight.

By morning, the grain had begun to ferment, and the 1,500-pound mountain was held together loosely by the growing *Aspergillus* mold. The grains were then separated through a hand-rubbing process in which the cooler rice on the surface of the mound was mixed with the warmer rice from the bottom. Usually four people performed this step, bending over the low table, sliding their open hands over the warm rice or barley, and working in a rhythm. They started at one end of the mound in the early morning, and by the afternoon, they had worked their way to the other end. This timeless ritual offered an amazing sight—people huddled around the low table, working in silence over the steaming koji. With hair that was covered with scarves, the workers stopped only occasionally to comment on their progress or to wipe the perspiration from their faces. To

Itsuko Onozaki (center), Jan (right), and Japanese coworker break up koji under the intense heat and humidity of the koji room.

John (right) and Miso Master Takamichi Onozaki scrape the finished koji from boxes.

our surprise, this job became a labor of love for us. We welcomed the ever-changing sweet smell of fermenting rice or barley, as well as the soothing warmth we felt when putting our cold hands into the warm grains on frosty winter mornings. Most of all, we derived much satisfaction from working with nature to produce a delicious living food.

After the grain was mixed and separated, it was put in small wooden boxes that were placed around the walls of the koji room in "bricklap" stacks—an arrangement that encouraged proper air circulation. Temperature and humidity, both very important to good koji growth, were regulated by the opening and closing of ceiling vents throughout the night. By morning, the surface of the grains was covered with a fine delicate web of glistening threads. The koji was mature.

Attention then turned to preparing the beans. About 1,500 pounds of hand-selected soybeans were washed, cooked, cooled, and crushed by late morning. Then Takamichi-san's wife, guided by years of experience, directed

the mixing of the crushed beans with koji, salt, and water to make unfermented ("raw") miso. Each 120-pound batch was divided in four buckets and relayed to a person standing on a ladder atop a huge six-ton-capacity cedar vat. With a loud thud, the first few batches hit the bottom of the empty vat. Within two or three hours, the seven-foot-tall vat was almost full.

The slow fermentation process began almost immediately. Some miso masters added 5 to 10 percent of their mature miso—called *seed miso*—as a catalyst to start fermentation. Takamichi Onozaki did not; he relied on the bacteria already present in his 200-year-old vats. For generations, these bacteria had been naturally selected; they were strong and well adapted for miso fermentation. Aided by enzymes in the koji, the bacteria started the long, natural fermentation of the soybeans and rice. Proteins and oils were gradually digested into simple amino and fatty acids. As the miso darkened, a delicious, almost black liquid called tamari gathered in pools around the inside of the vat. The rapidly multiplying bacterial population, eager for a source of food to support its growing numbers, converted complex car-

John prepares to cook soybeans in 400-gallon cooker.

Jan places river rocks
atop four tons of
fermenting miso at
Onozaki miso shop.

bohydrates into maltose, glucose, ethyl alcohol, and organic acids, giving off a deep, rich aroma that filled the room.

Under the natural conditions of the open storage room, the fermentation rate adjusted to the changing seasons. Lying almost dormant in the winter, bacteria were gradually awakened by the warmth of spring, and then stimulated into a frenzy in the heat of summer. Takamichi-san's miso had the benefit of at least two summers.

Each day after work, we ate dinner together and then talked or studied for a few hours. We then took hot baths before settling into our futons. By 10:30, only the cats playing on the roof disturbed the tranquility of the darkened house. Like a mantra, the calming effects of our daily life gave us strength and peace of mind. It was a natural rhythm, a reflection of nature, like the slow rising and falling of breath during deep meditation.

As fall turned to winter and the temperature of the unheated house dropped below 0°C, a heated table—the *kotatsu*—became the center of our nightlife. It was on one such night toward the end of our stay, while huddled together on the living room floor, that Takamichi-san showed us his ancient family scroll. Beginning on the east coast of Japan around 1200 AD, it recorded the birth, life, and death of each first-born son of the Onozaki family, down to Takamichi-san's father, who had died just two years earlier. In ancient script, it told of the family's early farming existence, its gradual ascent to samurai lordship, and the continuous struggle to maintain its domain against overwhelming forces. A blank space, reserved for Takamichi-san, was at the far end of the scroll. Takamichi had no sons; he was the last Onozaki. This was, no doubt, on his mind as he shared this family treasure with us.

Not long before we prepared to return to America with our new craft, Tamagachi-san presented us with a beautiful black-lacquered box that had a picture of his kin's coat of arms on the lid. We believed it was his way of saying that he considered us a small, ongoing part of his family.

2. Miso Medicine

Touted for centuries in the Far East as a folk remedy for poor digestion, cancer, tobacco poisoning, acidic conditions, low libido, and several types of intestinal infections, miso has long had a reputation as one of nature's most healing foods. By the end of the twentieth century, scientific studies had confirmed this reputation. It is miso's combination of ingredients and its unique double-fermentation process that transforms soybeans and grains into a potent medicine.

MISO AND WESTERN AWARENESS

Western awareness of miso largely began during the late 1960s when Michio Kushi and Hermann Aihara, students of Japanese teacher and writer George Ohsawa, spearheaded the macrobiotic movement in the United States. The macrobiotic philosophy, which promotes balance in all aspects of life, places emphasis on a diet that includes foods such as whole grains, land and sea vegetables, nuts, seeds, pickles, and miso. Macrobiotics played a significant role in introducing miso to a health-conscious public.

During the 1960s, students of macrobiotics and Zen began to learn of Dr. Shinichiro Akizuki, the Director of the Department of Internal Medicine at Saint Francis Hospital in Nagasaki

during the Second World War. After the atomic bombing of Japan in 1945, Dr. Akizuki, spent years treating patients who developed symptoms of radiation sickness from the fallout. He fed his patients and staff a strict daily diet that included miso soup. Although they were located only one mile from ground zero, the progressive effects of radiation never manifested. Akizuki hypothesized that the miso soup is what offered the protection.

In 1972, researchers discovered that miso contains *dipilocolonic acid*, an alkaloid that chelates (binds together) heavy metals, such as radioactive strontium, and discharges them from the body. This discovery helped validate Akizuki's theory that miso offered protection against radiation exposure. More convincing evidence came in 1989 through the research of Professor Akihiro Ito at Hiroshima University's Atomic Radioactivity Medical Lab. A few years earlier in April of 1986, the world's worst nuclear disaster occurred at a power plant in Chernobyl in the former Soviet Union (now the Ukraine). European countries imported truckloads of miso from Japan and fed it to their people as protection against the radioactive fallout. This prompted Professor Ito to conduct studies on miso's effects on irradiated laboratory rats. One group of rats was fed a diet that included miso; the other group's diet did not. The rats that were not fed miso had a liver cancer rate that was 100 to 200 percent higher than the rats in the miso-fed group. Ito also reported that the organs of the miso-fed rats were much less inflamed than those in the other group.

OTHER EARLY STUDIES

Although Ito's studies were very impressive, the large, long-term population studies that were conducted in Japan during the 1960s and 1970s first alerted researchers to miso's potential as a potent medicinal food. One of these studies, which included over 250,000 men and women, indicated that those who ate miso soup every day had fewer cases of certain types of cancer. The results also showed a much lower incidence of coronary heart disease, liver cirrhosis, cerebrovascular disease, and peptic ulcers among those who ate miso soup.

In the late 1980s, a team of medical researchers at Japan's Tohoku University discovered that miso contains an *ethyl ester*—a fatty acid produced during fermentation that acts as an *anti-mutagen*. Through this work, researchers learned that the ethyl ester in miso is made only during fermentation, and the small amounts that are ingested in miso soup could cancel the harmful effects of nicotine and mutagens from charred or burnt meat.

Another population study conducted by the University of Alabama at Birmingham, compared breast cancer rates among first-generation Japanese women who immigrated to Hawaii with subsequent generations. The study showed the first-generation group had a 40-percent lower breast cancer rate than the generations that followed. Researchers theorized that the typical Japanese diet, which includes miso, natto, soy sauce, and other fermented soy foods, may have been responsible for the lower cancer rate among the first-generation group, whose

consumption of these foods in Japan was higher than later generations.

The results of another study involving over 20,000 Japanese women were published in the June 2003 issue of *Journal of the National Cancer Institute*. The study showed that miso's preventive effects against breast cancer increased with daily consumption. For the group that ate three bowls a day, the breast cancer rate was 40 percent lower. The study concluded that "consumption of miso soup and isoflavones, was inversely associated with the risk of breast cancer." Interestingly, the study found miso specifically to be more effective in breast cancer prevention than soy foods in general. The likely reason is that some soy foods are not very high in cancer-fighting isoflavones, detailed in the following discussion.

ISOFLAVONES
SOY FOOD'S SILVER BULLET

During the 1990s, an explosion of exciting research pointed to the extraordinary health benefits of soy foods in general and miso in particular. Population studies in Japan, China, and Singapore linked lower rates of several types of cancer, including kidney, uterine, breast, ovarian, and prostate cancer, with the consumption of traditional soy foods. This prompted scientists around the world to find the silver bullet in miso, tofu, soymilk, soy sauce, tempeh, and even textured vegetable protein (TVP). They discovered that these foods contained a high concentration of a potent anticancer agent called *genistein,* a plant isoflavone.

According to an article from the National Cancer Institute and research from Children's University Hospital in Heidelberg, Germany, genistein delivers a one-two punch to cancer cells. It reduces the cell's ability to form new blood vessels, a process called *angiogenesis;* it also attacks the cell's reproduction mechanism. Without a growing blood supply or the ability to generate new cells, the cancer cells slowly shrink and die.

Numerous studies have demonstrated genistein's ability to destroy cancer cells, both in and out of the body. When added to cultures of skin cancer cells, as reported in the *British Journal of Cancer*, genistein rapidly suppressed growth of the cells, which began to die. And in several dietary studies in which animals with various forms of cancer were fed miso, the results were the same—and clearly dose dependent. The more miso in the diet, the more effective it was in slowing or stopping the cancer growth.

Genistein also helps prevents cancer cell growth either by inhibiting or activating cancer-related genes in the body. It inhibits, for example, the activity of certain enzymes created by *oncogenes*—genes that trigger the development of some cancer types. Genistein also activates certain genes that trigger cancer cells to self-destruct.

Scientists believe that genistein, like several other plant compounds called *phytoestrogens*, may be effective on both hormonal and non-hormonal cancers. Because of their similar molecular structure to human estrogens, phytoestrogens can work in two ways. They can block the effects of too much estrogen, alleviating certain symptoms, such as those affiliated with premenstrual syndrome (PMS). And when estrogen levels are low, as they are during and after menopause, soy phytoestrogens bind to vacant estrogen receptors and help relieve common symptoms such as mood swings and hot flashes. High levels of estrogen have also been linked to breast, ovarian, uterine, and cervical cancers. By blocking estrogen uptake, genistein and other isoflavones may help prevent these hormone-related cancers.

In the mid 1990s, the National Cancer Institute recommended miso and other soy foods containing isoflavones to help protect against breast and prostate cancer. In addition, the consumption of soy foods and isoflavones has also been positively linked to improved mental function, stabilized blood sugar levels in diabetics, and protection against osteoarthritis. This interest and excitement over isoflavones has resulted in a flood of both natural and synthetic genistein supplements; however, miso is one of its most concentrated natural sources.

What is it about the soybean that gives it such incredible healing power? The answer may be attributed to its abundance of isoflavones, including genistein and daidzein, which serve as natural pesticides. Dr. James Duke, USDA botanist and well-known herbal authority, hypothesizes that the soybean's abundant natural fungicides work together synergistically to enhance their medicinal effects on humans. In protecting the soybean from its natural enemies, nature may have provided mankind with one of its most effective medicinal foods.

THE ROLE OF FERMENTATION

Isoflavones are found in most soy products, even TVP; however, *miso has about twenty times more isoflavones than unfermented soy foods*, like soymilk and tofu. Why? The answer lies in miso's fermentation process, which increases isoflavone concentration. Even soybeans that have fermented for as little as four months have significantly high levels of isoflavones. A group of USDA scientists confirmed this belief when they compared amounts of the isoflavones genistein and daidzein in a wide variety of foods and plants. Their report, which appeared in *Journal of Alternative Complementary Medicine*, stated that the level of these isoflavones was thirty times higher in fermented soybeans (soybean miso) than in the same amount of dry beans.

Furthermore, numerous studies have shown that fermentation of foods with lactobacilli increases the quantity, availability, digestibility, and assimilability of nutrients while promoting a healthy pH in the digestive system. What's more, lactobacillus fermentation kills dangerous pathogens in foods both before they are eaten and in the intestinal tract. One study, published in the *Annals of Medicine,* reports the effective use of freeze-dried lactobacillus bacteria for the treatment of salmonellosis, shigellosis, and antibiotic-induced diarrhea. This explains why these types of fermented foods are used in third world countries to prevent and treat various intestinal infections.

Beneficial bacteria found in the small intestine are also effective in fighting conditions such as constipation, yeast infections (candidiasis), and lactose intolerance. Now research is beginning to suggest that some friendly bacterial strains may combat more serious diseases such as coronary heart disease and cancer.

When the air we breathe, the food we eat, the water we drink, and the drugs we take upset the delicate ratio of friendly to dangerous bacteria in our digestive system, enzymes are produced that can change normal by-products of digestion into cancer-causing toxins. Moreover, once cancer is established in the body, friendly bacteria can help destroy tumor cells. Regularly eating foods high in these microorganisms, such as unpasteurized miso, can help maintain a healthy balance of bacteria in your digestive tract.

Proponents of the macrobiotic diet have advocated the importance of the probiotic effects of unpasteurized miso for decades. George W. Yu, M.D., clinical professor of urology at George Washington University Medical Center, has presented to the National Cancer Institute several case histories of terminal cancer patients who have failed conventional treatment, but have found success using the macrobiotic diet as the main treatment. Dr. Yu believes it may be the probiotic influence of the microorganisms in foods such as miso that is responsible for their anti-cancer effects.

A LINK TO LOWERED CHOLESTEROL

Coronary heart disease (CHD) is the most common form of heart disease and the number-one cause of death in the United States. In October of 1999, the Food and Drug Administration (FDA) authorized manufacturers of foods that contained soy protein to state on product labels that the foods help reduce the risk of coronary heart disease. This decision was based on the findings of over fifty scientific studies in which soy protein was linked to the lowering of both total blood cholesterol and low-density lipoproteins (LDLs), or "bad" cholesterol—both proven risk factors for CHD. Studies have also shown that consuming twenty-five grams of soy protein per day supplies enough isoflavones to lower cholesterol levels. This is about the same amount of isoflavones found in $1\frac{1}{2}$ teaspoons of miso, the quantity used to make just one cup of miso soup.

Besides lowering cholesterol directly, soy isoflavones may reduce blood clotting, reducing the risk of heart attack and stroke. They may also prevent the multiplication of cells that make up artery plaque. Other ingredients found in soybeans and miso can also play a role in managing blood cholesterol levels. In fact, soybeans are one of nature's best sources of lecithin and linolenic acid, which play an important role in cholesterol metabolism.

MISO AND BLOOD PRESSURE

High blood pressure, which increases the risk of stroke and heart and kidney disease, is a serious public health concern for millions of Americans. In addition to risk factors such as obesity, genetics, and diet, the high sodium content of food has also been implicated in elevated blood pressure. Foods that are considered high in sodium, such as miso, are typically not recommended for those concerned with their blood pressure. However, concern about dietary sodium may actually be a "red herring." Recent medical research and traditional wisdom agree that it is not the amount of sodium in the diet that is important but rather the balance of minerals such as potassium, magnesium, calcium, and

sodium in the body. In fact, research has shown that adding potassium to the diet, which helps relax blood vessels and remove sodium from the blood, can be as effective in lowering blood pressure as reducing sodium intake.

Miso soup made with foods that are high in potassium, magnesium, and calcium, such as wakame, fish stock (bonito), greens, and carrots, has been shown to actually lower high blood pressure, as well as prevent it from occurring in people with normal rates. A four-year study of elderly Japanese men and women with normal blood pressure, conducted by the School of

Lowering High Cholesterol
Conventional Medicine or Miso?

One in five Americans has high cholesterol, and treating it has become a billion-dollar industry. The most frequently prescribed medications for high cholesterol, the statin drugs Lipitor and Zocor, are not always effective, even when prescribed with dietary recommendations and exercise. They are also expensive—today's average cost is about $150 a month. Furthermore, these medications come with possible side effects, the most common being abdominal pain, abnormal heartbeat, back pain, indigestion, leg cramps, constipation, and fatigue. (One product lists over seventy side effects!) More serious side effects can include liver and muscle damage. Moreover, these drugs should not be taken by children, pregnant women, or those who are breastfeeding. Nor should they be taken in combination with antacids, antibiotics, oral contraceptives, and certain vitamins.

An effective alternative to these medications is miso—a safer, much less expensive means of

lowering cholesterol. And its only side effect besides better health is a sense of calm and well-being. For many, a daily bowl of miso soup is all that is necessary to see results, often within a short period of time. Reported cases in which cholesterol levels were high—in the over-300 range—have shown a 25 to 40 percent reduction in only three or four months! (In many cases, miso was part of an overall natural foods diet.) Furthermore, miso soup tastes good! Adding some shiitake mushrooms, wakame, tofu, and vegetables enhances its flavor and medicinal value even further. We personally know of cases in which cholesterol levels dropped so dramatically that the physicians could not believe the results and retested to be certain.

For lowering cholesterol, you have a choice. Either take conventional medication with its limitations and possible side effects or simply incorporate miso soup into your daily diet. The decision is yours.

Medicine, Showa University, showed that two daily bowls of miso soup made with the right combination of ingredients can prevent the development of high blood pressure. Another thirteen-year study of a large population of Japanese men and women showed that those who abstained from miso soup had a death rate from high blood pressure three and a half times higher than miso soup drinkers! Other studies have credited the daily use of miso with reduced risk of stroke, which is often associated with high blood pressure.

It is ironic that medical science, while advocating the use of foods that are low in sodium, prescribes blood pressure medications such as diuretics, which cause the body to lose potassium among other side effects. For most people, there's a simpler solution than being overly concerned with sodium intake. That is, eating a balanced unrefined diet that is naturally high in potassium and other mineral-rich foods, such as miso soup.

A SOURCE OF ANTIOXIDANTS

Antioxidants, which neutralize damaging free radicals in the body, are extremely important for fighting disease and the signs of aging, as well as boosting overall health. Air pollution, radiation generated from televisions and computers, drugs, alcohol, poor diet, chemicals, and stress generate free radicals, which attack the body's cellular structures. Because free radicals are missing an electron, they steal them from healthy molecules, creating even more free radicals in the body. The damaging result can be degenerative disease, bacterial and viral infections, and accelerated aging. It's important for our bodies to produce enough antioxidants to get rid of these damaging free radicals.

Miso is a rich source of antioxidants. The soybean, miso's basic component, contains known antioxidants, including vitamin E; *saponins*, cholesterol-like plant compounds; and *melanoidins*, the dark pigment responsible for the color of long-aged miso. In a study conducted at Japan Women's University in Tokyo, scientists attributed miso's antioxidative properties to its dark pigments. Another study at the University of Shizuoka in Japan, identified daidzein, genistein, and alpha-tocopherol as the active antioxidants in miso. Yet another Japanese study identified a "potent" antioxidative substance in the koji component of miso. Other substances produced during fermentation may also play a role in protecting against free radical damage.

MISO AND BREAST CANCER

According to current United States health statistics, one out of every eight women will develop breast cancer. In Japan, where women consume a diet rich in soy foods such as tofu and miso, the breast cancer rate is 400 percent lower! Most research has focused on soy's anti-estrogen properties. As discussed earlier in this chapter, estrogen can stimulate the growth of breast cancer cells. Soy isoflavones, however, can block the estrogen, reducing the size of existing cancer cells or even preventing them from forming.

Like soy, medications such as tamoxifen interfere with the activity of estrogen and have been used for decades to successfully treat patients with breast cancer. Researchers in the Department of Cancer Research at Japan's Hiroshima University combined miso with tamoxifen to treat animals with mammary cancer. They found this combination to have a powerful synergistic effect. "These results," researchers reported in the *Japanese Journal of Cancer Research*, "indicate that miso is useful in protecting against mammary cancer, and it can be expected to have a potent anti-tumor effect, especially when used in combination with tamoxifen."

MISO AND CHRONIC PAIN REDUCTION

According to unpublished clinical studies conducted by Mark Young, M.D., professor of physical medicine and rehabilitation at Johns Hopkins Medical School, miso is effective for reducing pain. Dr. Young reports, "I have had tremendous anecdotal success recommending miso and dulse flakes to my chronic pain patients. Since miso soup is an excellent source of some B vitamins, beta carotene, calcium, iron and magnesium, I postulate that miso soup is likely a valuable 'pain modulater' by optimizing several critical metabolic and biochemical reactions." In his book *Women and Pain: Why It Hurts and What You Can Do* (Hyperion, 2002), Dr. Young attributes miso's prominence in the macrobiotic diet to its concentrated protein content and anti-carcinogenic properties. "As a by-product, pain relief may result," states Young.

Several of Dr. Young's colleagues at Johns Hopkins have been studying the role of soy in pain management. In 2000, they presented their findings to the American Pain Society in Baltimore, concluding that soy's "anti-inflammatory benefits" resulted in pain reduction.

MISO AND FOOD ALLERGIES

Food allergies are usually an immune response to proteins. Allergists now know that it is the complex proteins in foods that cause the body's immune system to trigger an immune response. Miso is known to contain *proteolytic enzymes*, which degrade complex proteins, rendering them much less allergenic. As miso ferments, or ages, the enzymes supplied by the koji digest the proteins of the rice, barley, and soybeans (depending on what type of miso is being made) into less complex amino acids. Not only are these amino acids much less allergenic, they are also much easier to digest and assimilate. In other words, the allergenic soy, rice, and barley proteins are destroyed by miso's fermentation process.

Furthermore, miso's hypoallergenic properties attribute to its effectiveness as a food tenderizer. For centuries, Japanese chefs have used miso marinades to tenderize fish, poultry, and meat. Miso's powerful enzymes break down the complex muscle and fat fibers of animal tissues and at the same time increase their ability to absorb flavors during the marinating and cooking process. For vegetarians, this same principle applies to making plant foods much more digestible and less allergenic. Foods that are high in protein and fiber, such as legumes and whole grains (particularly wheat), can cause allergic reactions and, more commonly, gastric distress, unless their complex protein is denatured. However, simple cooking may not be enough, particularly for sensitive individuals. Simply adding unpasteurized "live" miso to a recipe can make a difference. Marinating tofu in miso marinade, for example, will make it more digestible, less allergenic, and more flavorful.

The powerful enzymatic action of miso, however, can also work against the unwary chef. When adding miso to recipes that are thickened with starches, such as kuzu powder, the miso must be added earlier and simmered for several minutes, because enzymes in unpasteurized miso tend to counteract the effects of thickening agents.

For decades, anecdotal references suggesting that unpasteurized miso contains important "living enzymes" had no scientific basis. However, like many of miso's medicinal properties, its remarkable ability to make some foods more acceptable to our immune and digestive systems, while improving their flavor and texture, is being confirmed by the scientific community.

MISO AND ENHANCED IMMUNE FUNCTION

Misos that are made with a large proportion of soybeans and usually aged for one year or longer, such as Hatcho, barley, brown rice, and soybean misos, are high in *arginine*, an important amino acid. Arginine retards the growth of tumors and cancer by enhancing the body's immune function. Those suffering from diseases, such as AIDS and other cancers that are caused by suppressed immune function, may find these long-term miso varieties beneficial. Arginine also has an important positive influence on liver function, sterility in men, weight loss, hormonal balance, and stimulation of the pancreas to release insulin.

MISO AND OSTEOPOROSIS

Some reports of osteoporosis in people who have a long history of eating a dairy-free natural food diet have caused some concern in the natural foods community. Although health statistics for people eating a mostly vegetable based diet are good, cases of low bone density have been reported. Since Americans get about 70 percent of their calcium requirements from dairy products, some nutritionists assume that low bone density is caused by the absence of dairy products in vegan diets. However, according to a report published by the Japan Federation of Miso Manufacturers Cooperative, almost 90 percent of the calcium in the traditional Japanese diet comes from non-dairy sources, particularly miso soup.

A bowl of miso soup with tofu, sea vegetables, and a little fish contains about 233 milligrams of calcium. What's more, miso is known to facilitate the absorption of calcium and other minerals. Eating miso along with other high calcium foods can be an alternative

A Nutritional Powerhouse

Miso is a good source of iron, calcium, phosphorus, potassium, some B vitamins, and protein. Since soybeans contain high amounts of protein, including all of the essential amino acids, miso varieties that are made primarily from soybeans, such as Hatcho miso, are considered an important source of complete protein. This is especially important for those eating a vegan diet. Miso also facilitates the body's absorption of calcium and magnesium.

A combination of miso and tofu in spreads, dips, and salad dressings, for example, is easily digested, delicious, and loaded with nutrition. Just one four-ounce serving of Creamy Dill Dip (page 54) contains the following percentages of the United States Recommended Daily Allowances (RDSs) of protein, vitamins, and minerals:

Protein–20% · Thiamin–4%
Calcium–12% · Niacin–4% · Iron–16%

The FDA, which has strict guidelines for nutritional labeling, considers a single serving of food that contains 10 percent of the RDA of protein "high" in protein. For vegetarians, dishes that combine miso and tofu can be an important source of protein and amino acids. Moreover, since the essential amino acids in soybeans and grains complement each other, the amount of protein that can be utilized by the body is increased.

to using medications that increase bone density. In fact, the isoflavone daidzein, which is found in soybeans, is very similar to ipriflavone, a drug used throughout Europe and Asia to treat osteoporosis.

MISO AS A NATURAL ANTACID

There is a great deal of anecdotal information regarding miso's ability to quickly soothe an acid stomach. Scientists have reported that miso has a strong buffer activity due to the presence of protein, peptides, amino acids, phosphoric acid, and various organic acids that are produced during the fermentation process. In the stomach, these buffers can reduce excess acidity and provide quick gastrointestinal relief. Scientists have also reported that miso's buffering ability is partly responsible for its important role as a seasoning. When mixed with foods, such as tomatoes and other acidic products, miso not only buffers the acids, it mellows the flavor.

MISO AND ESSENTIAL FATTY ACIDS

Of the approximately fifty known essential nutrients, essential fatty acids (EFAs) contain the highest daily requirements. Unlike other fats, the EFAs *linolenic acid* and *linoleic acid* are precursors to hormone-like substances that regulate vital processes, such as blood pressure, immunity, inflammation, cholesterol level, cell growth, neural impulses, and reproduction. EFA balance can also affect emotional states, influencing such feelings as love, sexiness, anger, and depression.

Dry soybeans, which are about 20 percent oil, are an excellent source of high-quality polyunsaturated fats, such as EFAs. Most of the soy oil sold in the United States, however, is made through a process that destroys most of the delicate EFAs. The daily use of soybean miso, which is made with only soybean koji, and water, is an excellent as well as flavorful way to get EFAs in your diet. In fact, misos such as Hatcho and "mame" are about 10 percent oil, of which 60 percent is a combination of linolenic and linoleic acids.

EFFECTIVENESS OF MISO'S BROWN PIGMENT

As miso ages, soy proteins are broken down and react with sugar to produce the dark pigments that give some long-aged varieties their characteristic brown and russet colors. When scientists at Aichi-Gakuin University Hospital, located in Nagoya, Japan, isolated the brown pigments in miso and soy sauce, referred to as *melanoidins*, and mixed them with human colon cancer cells, the growth rate of the cells was cut in half. Moreover, closer examination showed that brown pigments disrupted cell growth during very specific phases of cell reproduction. In another study with animals, brown pigments showed a strong scavenging activity against free radicals.

BENEFITS OF LONGER-AGED MISO VARIETIES

Many, but not all, of miso's health-promoting and disease-fighting biochemicals such as essential fatty acids, lecithin, saponins, isoflavones, and melanoidins come from its fermented soybean component. Since long-aged misos such as Hatcho, red, barley, and brown rice miso are made with more soybeans than short-aged mellow and sweet misos, it makes sense that longer-aged misos have greater medicinal properties than shorter-aged varieties. Studies at

Miso, Macrobiotics, and Chinese Medicine

Miso's growing popularity in the West is partly due to the important role it plays in the practice of macrobiotics and Chinese medicine. Asheville, North Carolina acupuncturist, macrobiotic counselor, and former dean of Atlantic University of Chinese Medicine in Mars Hill, North Carolina, Michael Rossoff draws on his thirty-five years of experience as a health practitioner to explain the health benefits of miso from his unique perspective:

"Miso is a powerful food for enhancing the immune system, blood quality, and digestive strength. From a macrobiotic perspective, miso soup has a natural alkalinity that aids the small intestines during the final stages of digestion and absorption. This alkaline soup, with sea vegetables, is replicating the ocean world, which represents the primitive origins of organic life. The primordial nature of the small intestines is central to our physical and mental health. This region, call *hara* in Japanese, means vital center. This center can become weak due to long-time consumption of acid forming foods such as simple sugars. One benefit of miso soup is that it stimulates the digestive juices, particularly the pancreatic enzymes. Since soup is eaten at the beginning of the meal, this effect helps prepare the digestive system for the diverse foods that will follow. On the subtle psychological and emotional levels, this all adds up to a strengthening of mental clarity, a calming of the emotions, and an improving of personal resolve.

In Chinese medicine all herbs and foods are classified by their flavor and associated organ system that they influence. Miso is considered to contain sweet, neutral, and salty flavors. The sweet and neutral flavors indicate that miso has a tonifying effect to the stomach and spleen. These organs, which are paired in Chinese medicine, are central to the body-mind's well-being. They control the entire digestive function. Further, the spleen functions to transform the energies inherent in all foods into our human blood. In this way, Chinese medicine says that blood is created by the power of the spleen. And the spleen is strengthened by miso, which, therefore, helps create strong blood.

When there is a loss of appetite, miso will quickly help restore interest in foods. This tonic effect will be enhanced because the soup is served warm or hot. The heat aids in the revitalizing of the stomach, just as cold always has an inhibiting effect.

Miso is also a natural detoxifier from food poisoning. This is partly due to its sweet and salty flavors. The sweet stimulates digestion, which helps activate the liver and gall bladder, another organ pair in Chinese medicine. These organs, especially the liver, can neutralize many food poisons. The salty flavor focuses to the kidneys, which, among its many functions, has the ability to quickly cleanse toxins from the blood.

The salty flavor in miso benefits the kidneys in another way. The kidneys are called the Gate of Life, since they store original essence and provide the core yin (cool) and yang (hot) energies of the body. Miso enhances and supports both of the core forces. Keeping the Gate of Life vital benefits all of our body systems."

Hiroshima University in Japan have confirmed this hypothesis.

When long- and short-aged misos were compared in animal dietary studies on radiation exposure and colon, lung, and stomach cancers, the long-aged misos were more effective in preventing these conditions. These results indicate that at least for some cancers and radiation sickness, long-aged misos are a healthier choice. Shorter-aged misos were also effective in these studies, only less so. They have their own unique benefits, such as a higher concentration of some vitamins, simple sugars, and lactobacillus bacteria.

It is not always possible to tell the type of miso you are purchasing from the name on the package. For example, although the words "red," "barley," and "brown rice" miso are on the label, and usually indicate long-aged misos, this is not always the case. Manufacturers, however, are required by law to list the ingredients in their miso by weight in descending order. To be sure you are getting long-aged miso, just check the ingredient list to be sure soybeans are listed before the rice or barley.

WHAT CONSTITUTES A HEALTHY DOSE?

If you want to experience miso's health benefits, it is essential that you eat it often. Population studies documenting the benefits of miso were done in Japan, where miso was historically eaten every day. Moreover, many of these studies were done decades ago when miso consumption was much higher than it is today. Compared to the Japanese, Americans eat very little miso.

There are no studies documenting the minimum amount of miso required in the diet to achieve some of the health benefits cited in this chapter; however, many laboratory experiments and human population studies have shown that some of these benefits are dose related—the more miso that is eaten, the better the results. For healthy adults, one cup of miso soup a day, ideally made with shiitake, tofu, wakame or kombu dashi, and two or three vegetables, should be enough to promote good health. (See "Ultimate Miso Soup" on page 85.) Although dark, long-aged miso should be used to make miso soup most of the year, in the summer or in warmer climates, sweet and mellow miso can be used with lighter vegetables in miso soup. Those who are suffering from a chronic degenerative disease or who have a family history of cancer or heart disease may want to consider—after consulting with a health care professional—eating two bowls of dark miso soup a day. For those in good health who want to use miso more than once a day, we recommend, in addition to a bowl of soup, enjoying a second serving of miso in a dip, salad dressing, or sauce.

LET TRADITION BE YOUR GUIDE

Besides the documented reports and research cited in this chapter, we have personally experienced the benefits of miso along with our friends and family. After researching material for over 120 articles and four books about food, we are confident that using miso regularly is the best health insurance you can have.

Much more than the proverbial "apple a day," a daily bowl of miso soup will not only keep the doctor away, it will add vitality to your life. Without a doubt, miso is a culinary treasure—the world's most medicinal everyday food.

Breakfast of Emperors
Making Miso in a Traditional Factory

In central Japan's Aichi Province in the town of Okazaki, a curious group of tile-roofed buildings stands proudly on 8th (Hatcho) Street. These buildings are home to the Hatcho Miso Company, Ltd., makers for five centuries of one of the country's true living treasures—the most revered miso in all Japan.

Under the ancient rafters of the shop stand rows of huge 200-year-old cedar vats that are held together with hoops of braided bamboo. Each vat is topped with a pressing lid on which sits a three-ton mountain of stones, so skillfully arranged that they will never collapse, even during earthquakes. Under the pressure of these stones, 12,000 pounds of Hatcho (pronounced hot-cho) miso ferments slowly and naturally through the hot, humid summers and mild Aichi winters. After twenty-four to thirty months, under the direction of eighteenth-generation president Kyuemon Hayakawa, workers remove the stones and pressing lid, exposing the rich, fragrant miso that has long been treasured by emperors, shoguns, and common people alike.

Hatcho Miso Company's rise to fame began in the late fifteenth century. Okazaki was the home of Japan's most famous warlord, Ieyasu Tokugawa, whose military exploits were popularized in the novel *Shogun* by James Clavell. In the shadows of Tokugawa's castle, a small soybean miso shop supplied the vital ingredient for the shogun's power breakfast.

Because of its concentrated nutrition and ability to keep for years, Tokugawa's miso was one of the most important military rations for his troops. After his army succeeded in conquering and unifying all of Japan, Tokugawa moved his headquarters to Tokyo, but contin-

The Hatcho Miso Company, maker for five centuries of Hatcho miso, the most revered miso in all of Japan.

ued to order miso from his hometown shop until his death. This official patronage as the "purveyor to the Shogun" guaranteed the Hatcho Miso Company its pre-eminent status, which it still enjoys today.

In 1892, Hatcho Miso Company received another, even more prestigious honor when it became purveyor to the emperor of Japan. Today, busloads of tourists visit the 8th Street shop to see where this legendary miso is made. However, you don't have to be a samurai or even live in Japan to enjoy Hatcho miso. Since 1971, the Mitoku Company, a Tokyo exporter of traditionally made Japanese foods, has exported this miso to natural foods distributors around the world.

Unlike other misos, which contain grains such as rice and barley, Hatcho miso is made only from whole soybeans, sea salt, a little roasted barley flour, and a small amount of water. A very concentrated source of nutrition, Hatcho miso contains 80 percent more protein and 20 to 25 percent less salt than long-aged rice and barley misos. It is an excellent source of essential amino acids, vitamins, and minerals; low in calories and fat; and packed with fiber.

Workers place the last few stones on a six-ton vat of Hatcho miso.

Considered an important medicinal food, miso's daily use is credited with numerous health benefits (see Chapter 2). Scientific research has suggested that much of miso's medicinal effects, particularly its anti-cancer properties, are related to its soybean component. For this reason, many alternative health providers specifically recommend soybean misos for the treatment and prevention of certain degenerative diseases.

Because Hatcho miso is made with very little water, it is dry compared to other misos, and can be packaged unpasteurized in sealed bags. Like yogurt, unpasteurized Hatcho miso is abundant in lactic acid bacteria and enzymes that aid digestion and food assimilation.

Although modern machines now do some of the work at Hatcho Miso Company, its basic production method has changed little in the last 500 years. First, premium Hokkaido soybeans are washed and soaked in water for an hour. The beans are then transferred to a 200-pound-capacity cooker, steamed for two hours, then left in the closed cooker overnight. This unusual cooking process gives Hatcho miso its deep cocoa brown color and characteristic smoky flavor.

The following morning, the soft, dark beans are crushed together in a special machine that then shapes them into two-inch crosses. The crosses are then lightly dusted with a mixture of *Aspergillus* spores and toasted barley flour, and left to incubate for forty-eight hours in a carefully controlled environment with the proper temperature and humidity. As the "hatcho crosses," now called *koji,* emerge from the incubation room, they are covered with a fragrant bloom of pale yellow mold and loaded with powerful digestive enzymes. The koji is mixed with sea salt and a small amount of water, and then transferred to one of the seven-foot-tall cedar vats.

When the vat is full, the miso is covered with a thick cotton cloth and pressing lid, which is

Rows of old cedar vats held together with bamboo hoops contain thousands of pounds of fermenting Hatcho miso.

then topped with a three-ton pyramid of stones. The unhurried process of natural aging begins. The enzymes supplied by the *Aspergillus* slowly mellow the mixture, transforming the complex protein, carbohydrates, and fats of the beans into dark, rich, flavorful amino and fatty acids and sweet simple sugars.

After at least two full years, the mature miso is scooped from the vats with a wooden shovel and then packaged. The best miso comes from deep down in the center of the vat. It was this miso that was traditionally presented to the emperors, who enjoyed Hatcho miso soup every day.

Although some manufacturers use the name Hatcho miso for their dark soybean misos, only the special miso made since the 1400s on 8th Street in the small town of Okazaki is authentic. The company's exacting ancient process gives this miso its savory aroma, mellow sweetness, and astringent flavor. According to brewmaster Kazuo Kuroda, the extreme pressure of the stones on the dry miso creates a low-oxygen environment that encourages the growth of Hatcho's special type of bacteria. What's more, over the centuries, a particular strain of *Aspergillus* mold, known as *Aspergillus hatcho,* has made its home in the cracks and crevices of the old seasoned vats and throughout the fermentation rooms on Hatcho Street. It gives the miso a unique flavor that cannot be duplicated by other miso makers.

Hatcho miso is a cultural artifact. More than most Japanese foods, it offers an authentic taste of old Japan.

3. Making Miso at Home

The growing popularity of miso has given rise to an interest it its home production, once a common Japanese practice. Now that dry koji (miso starter) is readily available in natural foods stores, increasing numbers of miso lovers are fermenting their own home brews. The process, though imbued with some mystique, is actually quite simple, requiring only four easily obtainable ingredients. Furthermore, the advantages of home processing include a 50 to 75 percent savings in cost, the opportunity to choose the best ingredients, and the sense of security and independence that comes with making your own high-quality fermented food.

Regardless of the type of miso you decide to make, the basic process is the same. Beans are cooked, crushed, and mixed with koji (grain inoculated with *Aspergillus* mold), sea salt, and water, and then placed in a container to ferment. Gradually, a rich, amber liquid—tamari—rises to the surface as powerful enzymes supplied by the koji, along with fermenting organisms from the environment, break down complex molecules in the beans into readily digestible amino acids, fatty acids, and simple sugars.

Table 3.1 on pages 32 and 33 presents ingredient amounts and fermentation times for three basic miso types. Type I is for a versatile sweet, light miso, which is excellent to use in creamy salad dressings, rich dips, and savory spreads. Usually called mellow miso, it is low in salt and matures in just four to eight weeks. Type II, which takes about three to four months to mature, is for an all-purpose, hearty miso with a moderate salt content. Type III is the variety usually imported from Japan. Dark and salty, it is great for savory soups and stews, and casseroles that include winter fare, such as root vegetables, winter squashes, and hardy greens like kale and collards. This type of miso must ferment for one year, or at least one entire summer. Although hundreds of varieties of miso are made in Japan, these three types represent the basic recipes used by traditional miso makers.

No matter which type you choose, the miso-making process is sure to be a rewarding experience, one that the entire family can enjoy. When our kids were young, they loved to get involved, helping to crush the beans and mix ingredients while we measured and cooked raw materials. As time passed and the fermenting miso matured, they would mimic us by placing their fingers in the bucket to sample the developing tamari. Finally, the day arrived when the stone was taken off the lid and the miso was uncovered. With excitement and anticipation, we would taste our homemade brew, usually deciding that it was the best we had ever made.

GETTING STARTED

To gain experience and confidence, we suggest that you first try your hand at mellow miso (Type I), which develops quickly. Make at least one full batch, or get together with friends to process even more (typically, the more you make, the better the results). It's also fine to make half batches on separate days and then mix them together. However, don't wait longer than one week between batches for short-term miso, and be sure to calculate fermentation time from when the last batch was added.

Plan to make miso on a day when you will have at least two uninterrupted hours. And keep in mind that the beans used in the process must first be soaked for twelve hours. Cooking the beans involves another time consideration. As you will see, depending on whether you use a pressure cooker or a pot, the beans can take anywhere from thirty minutes to four hours or more to cook.

Before starting, be sure to have all of the necessary utensils and ingredients, which are listed below. We also suggest reading through the procedure to familiarize yourself with the process. While making the miso, take notes. For instance, be sure to jot down the date the mixture was made and when you expect it to be mature. Also mark down anything you've observed that might influence the results of the final product. For instance, "the beans were overcooked" or "the mixture seems very wet." Subtle variations can make a noticeable difference in the miso.

WHAT YOU'LL NEED

Although the miso-making process is relatively simple, it's important to use the proper ingredients as well as the right tools and utensils to ensure success.

Utensils

The following checklist provides all of the items you'll need to make your homemade miso. Be sure to have everything on hand before starting.

❏ **Kitchen scale.** Used for weighing the dry beans, koji, and salt, this scale must have at least a five-pound capacity.

❏ **Pressure-cooker (7 quart) or pot.** To cook $2\frac{1}{2}$ pounds of dry beans, this size pot is needed. For more than $2\frac{1}{2}$ pounds, use either two pressure cookers, or cook the beans in two batches.

❏ **Oil skimmer or slotted spoon.** As the beans soak and as they cook, their hulls will loosen and float to the top. A skimmer or slotted spoon is ideal for removing the hulls.

❏ **Large colander or bamboo basket.** Needed for draining the beans after they have been soaked, and then again, after they are cooked.

❏ **Standard meat grinder or potato masher.** Used for crushing or puréeing the cooked beans.

❏ **Large mixing bowl.** Used for mixing together the salt and koji. The size of the bowl will depend on the amount of the ingredients called for in the specific recipe.

❏ **Mixing bowl (8 quart).** Used for combining the koji-salt mixture with the crushed beans. If you don't have a bowl of this size, mix the ingredients directly in the fermentation container (see below).

❏ **Measuring cup (1-quart).** Needed for measuring water and salt.

❏ **Large wooden spoon.** Used for combining the ingredients.

❏ **Fermentation container.** A leakproof wooden bucket, ceramic crock, or large plastic pail (the type that contains bulk tofu) is needed to store the miso mixture as it ferments. Large, wide-mouth glass jars are also appropriate. Never use metal containers unless they are stainless steel or enamel-coated. A 2-gallon container (9 inches in diameter and about 10 inches high) is perfect for a twelve- to fifteen-pound batch of miso, while a 5-gallon container (12 inches in diameter and about 15 inches high) is fine for a double batch of about twenty-four to thirty pounds.

The basic shape of the container should also be considered. Air that comes into contact with the fermenting miso adversely affects its quality. For this reason, try to choose a container that is taller than it is wide to minimize the surface area of the fermenting brew. Do not fill the container more than 80 percent, and be sure it is clean, particularly when made of wood. After rinsing the inside with boiling water, scrub wooden containers thoroughly with salt, using a stiff brush.

❏ **Clean white or natural cotton cloth.** Once the miso mixture has been put in the fermentation container, this piece of cloth is placed on top to cover the surface.

❏ **Sheet of clear plastic.** To help prevent moisture loss during the fermentation process, this plastic sheet is placed over the cotton cloth on the surface of the fermenting miso.

❏ **Pressing lid.** Set on top of the fermenting miso, a weighted lid is used to press the liquid (tamari) from the developing miso. The best pressing lids are flat pieces of wood that are cut round to fit inside the containers, or two layers of thin wood strips that are placed perpendicular to each other. Other good options include flat plates or lids from smaller plastic buckets. There should be at least $1/4$-inch space between the lid and the inner edge of the container.

Although all lids must be clean, wooden types should be scrubbed with salt and rinsed with boiling water. And avoid using wood that has been chemically treated, such as plywood or pressure-treated, rot-resistant outdoor wood.

❏ **Weight.** Placed on top of the pressing lid to weigh it down, the weight should equal 20 to 30 percent of the weight of the miso. Round, hard river stones make excellent and aesthetically pleasing weights. Bricks, tightly sealed containers of water, or jars filled with grains or beans work fine as well. Never use metal weights or soft stones, which will react adversely with the salty tamari and ruin the miso.

❏ **Piece of cloth and string.** To protect the fermenting miso from dust and insects, cover the entire top of the container, including the lid and weight, with a piece of cloth (or paper) and fasten it with string.

❏ **2 small wooden blocks.** For better, more even temperature control, the container should be placed on blocks to keep it off the floor. This is even more important if the container is made of wood, because leaving it on the ground could cause it to rot from the humidity.

Ingredients

Although the ingredients needed to make miso are simple and few, it's important that they are of high quality. In addition to proper manufacturing methods, good-quality ingredients are the most important factor in making good miso.

❏ **Beans.** Large, organically grown, light-colored soybeans with a light seam (hilum) are preferred for their thin skin and low oil content. Almost any soybeans that are sold in natural foods stores will do. You can create interesting tastes and colors for your homemade miso by using other legumes, such as pinto beans, garbanzo beans (chick peas), azuki beans, or black soybeans, either in addition to or instead of soybeans.

❑ **Koji.** The enzymatic starter for miso, koji is available in brown rice, white rice, and pearled barley varieties at well-stocked natural foods stores. It can also be special ordered in large quantities from natural foods distributors or through mail order companies. When making rice miso, it is important to use rice koji; barley miso requires barley koji. Store koji in a sealed container and refrigerate until ready to use.

❑ **Sea Salt.** Obtained from sea water through evaporation, sea salt is an important ingredient in miso. It contains important trace minerals like copper and zinc, which are lacking in commercial salt. Use only fine (ungranulated) sundried sea salt, not rock salt. Sold in natural foods stores, sea salt comes in many domestic varieties, as well as imported brands from Europe, Mexico, and Japan. All are fine to use.

❑ **Water.** Pure water is so important for making good miso that some traditional Japanese miso shops are actually built over wells of exceptional quality. For your homemade brew, use only untreated domestic water, spring water, or well water. Treated water or distilled water can actually retard the fermentation process.

❑ **Seed Miso.** Basically, seed miso is a sample from a batch of miso that has already been made, and then added to a new batch. Most miso makers take pride in the unique character of their miso. Specific strains of "wild" fermenting organisms give homemade miso exceptional flavor and aroma. To perpetuate this uniqueness, miso makers often add 5 to 10 percent of their mature miso (seed miso) to inoculate each new batch. This practice, called "seeding," also speeds up fermentation. You may wish to add seed miso to your own special blend. When preparing your first batch, add about half a cup of your favorite store-bought unpasteurized miso to the mixture. (This half-cup amount is appropriate for any of the recipes in Table 3.1 on pages 32 and 33.) For subsequent brews, use mature miso from your previous homemade batches.

GENERAL TIPS BEFORE STARTING

Although there is no greater teacher than personal experience, you should be aware of a few miso-making factors before starting. Temperature, climate, even the way in which the beans are cooked can influence the outcome of your efforts. Keeping the following tips in mind will help ensure success.

Cooking the Beans

The exceptional taste of high-quality miso will develop to its fullest only if the soybeans are properly cooked. To test, place a cooked soybean on a kitchen scale and crush it gently under one finger. It should crush evenly under 500 to 1,000 grams of pressure—that's about 18 to 36 ounces. Undercooked soybeans require more than 36 ounces of pressure before splitting, while overcooked beans, which are typically gray-colored and sticky, will crush under less than 18 ounces of pressure. Because undercooked soybeans will not ferment properly, it is better to err on the side of overcooking.

Moisture and Fermentation

Moisture content strongly influences the rate of miso fermentation. Wet miso ferments faster than dry. When freshly mixed miso is placed in the palm of your hand it should flow freely between your fingers as you gradually close

Tamari

Taking its name from the Japanese verb *tamaru*, which means "to accumulate or pool," tamari is the thick, rich, flavorful liquid that pools on the surface of fermenting miso. Miso tamari's sweet delicious flavor is different from store-bought soy tamari. If you are lucky enough to collect some from your homemade miso, use it like soy sauce in cooking and pickling.

Tamari plays an important role in miso making. It provides the liquid needed to drive the complex biological process of fermentation. A layer of tamari on the surface of the fermenting miso also helps prevent the miso from making contact with the air, especially during hot summer months. For short-term misos, which ferment rapidly, a pool of tamari is not essential. However, long-term miso should have at least one-eighth inch of tamari on its surface, especially during warmer months. Increasing the weight on the pressing lid will cause the tamari to rise to the surface. If you add too much water when preparing the miso mixture, as much as two inches of tamari may pool on the

---

your hand. Compare the feel of your unfermented miso to the store-bought variety sold in sealed plastic bags. Your miso should feel about the same or a little softer.

The most common error when preparing your own miso is to make it too dry. As you mix the ingredients, be sure to add the water slowly. When the consistency feels right, stop and let the mixture sit for about an hour. This will give the dry koji a chance to absorb the water. After an hour, check the consistency again. If it seems too dry, add more water. It is better to add a little too much water than not enough. However, be careful not to add too much water, as this can dilute the salt and result in improper fermentation.

Temperature, Climate, and Seasons

Miso is a living food. Its manufacture, like other agricultural activities, depends on natural climatic conditions and seasonal cycles. Miso's fermenting organisms lie dormant through winter and are gradually stimulated by the warmth of spring. It is the heat of summer, however, that produces a frenzy of fermentation, which is gradually subdued by cooler temperatures in the fall.

Long-term miso (Type III), with its higher salt and bean content, must ferment through at least one summer in temperate climates and two summers in very cold regions. It is best to make this type of miso in the late winter or early spring, before the weather begins to turn warm. This allows the mixture to take advantage of a full summer of intense fermentation.

Miso types that require less fermentation (Types I and II) contain less salt and beans, and proportionately more koji than long-fermenting varieties. Unless prepared in very cold regions, they do not require a full summer of fermentation. These types are best made in early fall or spring, when they can ferment at temperatures between 75°F and 80°F.

Natural temperatures are best for fermenting miso. Although artificial heating greatly accelerates the fermentation process, it can destroy the product's unique character. Large, commercially made volumes (1,000 pounds or more) can withstand 100°F for a short period,

Table 3.1. Recipe Guidelines for Basic Miso Types

The following table provides ingredient requirements and other necessary information for making six basic miso varieties. Standard among traditional miso makers, these varieties fall into one of three major

Description			Characteristics When Mature	
Type and Fermentation Length	Variety	Color	Taste	
Type I Short Term (4 to 8 weeks)	Mellow Barley Miso	Beige to yellow-brown	Mildly sweet, subtly tart, smoky	
	Mellow White Miso	Light beige to yellow	Mildly sweet, subtly tart	
Type II Mid Term (3 to 4 months)	Country Barley Miso	Beige to light brown	Rich and mellow with sweet/salty balance	
	Yellow Miso	Rich yellow to orange	Savory sweet, subtly tart	
Type III Long Term (1 year)	Barley Miso	Reddish brown to dark brown	Deep, rich saltiness with subtle sweetness	
	Rice (Red) Miso	Reddish brown to russet	Well-balanced with salty/tart sweetness	

but small homemade batches (20 to 100 pounds) should not stay in temperatures above 90°F for more than a few days.

Proper Aging

Since miso is such an important and vital food, it is essential to clearly understand which factors influence its taste, medicinal qualities, and nutritional value. By far, the most important factors are manufacturing methods and ingredient quality. If you choose high-quality ingredients and follow the guidelines outlined in this chapter, you will be well on the way to making good miso. However, there's another factor that plays an important role in a quality product—proper aging.

As you will discover, each miso type has its own character, which determines the proper amount of time it should age. Light miso (Type I) is not simply a dark miso recipe that has fermented for a short time. However, if light miso is fermented for too long, it *will* turn dark, lose its fresh sweet taste, and look very much like two-year-old dark miso in just a few months! During early fermentation, dark miso (Type III) is light in color but very salty and raw tasting. What's important to understand is that *proper* aging, not *longer* aging, is what actually determines the color, taste, and overall quality of miso. And the amount of time needed for proper aging depends on the particular recipe and climate.

After making a few batches of miso using the recipes in Table 3.1 above, you might want to try your hand at experimenting with your own variations. Although there is a wide range "types," which are categorized by their fermentation length. Use this information when following the procedure for making miso, which begins on the page below.

Fermentation Temperature	Ingredients				Approximate Yield
Fahrenheit Range	Dry Koji	Dry Beans	Sea Salt	Water	Volume and Weight*
75°–85°F	4 lbs. barley koji	2½ lbs.	13.6 oz. (2 cups)	4–6 cups	4 quarts (13 lbs.)
75°–85°F	4 lbs. white or brown rice koji	2½ lbs.	13.6 oz. (2 cups)	4–6 cups	4 quarts (13 lbs.)
75°–85°F	4 lbs. barley koji	3 lbs.	1 lb., 3 oz. (2¾ cups)	4–6 cups	4¼ quarts (14 lbs.)
75°–85°F	4 lbs. white or brown rice koji	3 lbs.	1 lb., 3 oz. (2¾ cups)	4–6 cups	4¼ quarts (14 lbs.)
75°–85°F	4 lbs. barley koji	4 lbs.	1 lb., 12 oz. (4 cups)	6–8 cups	5¼ quarts (17 lbs.)
75°–85°F	4 lbs. white or brown rice koji	4 lbs.	1 lb., 12 oz. (4 cups)	6–8 cups	5¼ quarts (17 lbs.)

*1 pound of miso is approximately 1 pint (2 cups)

of possibilities, the basic ratios of ingredients given in the table should not be altered radically. Just keep the following principle in mind: *Less salt and/or more koji speed up fermentation. Conversely, more salt, less koji, and/or more beans slow down fermentation.*

THE PROCEDURE FOR MAKING MISO AT HOME

To help familiarize yourself with the miso-making process, we recommend reading through the following steps before actually starting the procedure. Choose any of the recipes in Table 3.1 above (we recommend one of the short-term varieties to start with), and then get ready to make one of the world's most healthful and good-tasting foods.

COOKING THE BEANS

1. Wash the beans and soak them for about 12 hours at room temperature. The water should be 4 to 6 inches above the beans to allow for expansion. As the beans soak, remove any loose hulls that float to the surface.

2. Transfer the soaked beans to a colander or bamboo basket and let drain for 5 minutes.

3. Place the drained beans in a pressure cooker* and add enough water to cover the beans by about 2 inches. (For 2½ pounds of dry beans, use a 7-quart cooker. For larger amounts, use two pressure cookers, or divide the beans and cook them in two batches.) Do not overfill the cooker, as the loosened hulls may clog the release valve.

4. Bring the beans to a simmer with the lid ajar, and then continue to simmer uncovered for 5 minutes, skimming off any foam or hulls that appear on the surface. Cover the cooker and bring to pressure over medium-high heat, and then lower the heat and cook for 30 minutes. (Watch and listen carefully as the beans are coming up to pressure. As soon as the pressure is up, turn down the heat to prevent the beans from bubbling up and spilling over.) As the beans cook, check the release valve from time to time to be sure it isn't clogged.

5. At the end of cooking time, remove the pot from the heat and place it under cold running water to quickly reduce the pressure. When the pressure has returned to normal, open the cooker and test the beans for doneness. If the beans are too hard, boil them until soft or pressure-cook for another 5 minutes.

6. Transfer the cooked beans to a colander or bamboo basket and drain for 5 minutes.

If boiling the beans in a pot, add enough water to cover the beans by about 2 inches and cook for $3^1/_2$ to 4 hours, or until soft. Add more water as needed to keep the beans covered as they cook.

PREPARING THE MIXTURE

1. Purée the cooked beans by putting them through a meat grinder or thoroughly crushing them with a potato masher.

2. Place the salt and koji in a large bowl, and mix well with a wooden spoon or your hands.

3. In a separate large (8-quart) bowl or pail* thoroughly mix about $1/_4$ of the salted koji with about $1/_4$ of the crushed beans. Continue adding and combining salted koji and beans until it is all mixed.

4. Add the water slowly, stirring to mix well until the proper consistency is achieved. If using seed miso, dissolve it in half of the water before mixing with the bean-koji mixture. Add more water as needed (see guidelines under "Moisture and Fermentation" on page 30).

5. Sprinkle about $1/_2$ teaspoon sea salt on the bottom of the fermentation container. Add the miso mixture a little at a time, packing it firmly after each addition to expel any air pockets. Once all of the mixture has been added, smooth the surface. Sprinkle $1/_2$ teaspoon of sea salt on top, and gently rub it into the mixture using the back of a spoon.

6. Place a clean white or natural cotton cloth over the surface of the mixture, tucking in the ends between the inner edge of the container and the miso mixture. Next place a clean piece of clear plastic wrap over the cloth, tucking in the ends as well.

7. Place the pressing lid firmly on top of the plastic and add the appropriate amount of weight (20 to 30 percent of the weight of the miso mixture).

8. To prevent dust or insects from entering the miso as it ferments, cover the top of the container with cloth or paper and fasten it with string. Place the container on two small blocks in a dark, cool, clean environment.

If you do not have a container of this size, you can mix the salted koji and beans right in the fermentation container.

CHECKING THE PROGRESS

1. Along with any other notes you may have made, be sure to record the date the miso was made and when it is expected to mature.

2. After two weeks, check to see if any tamari has come to the surface. If it hasn't, add more weight and check again in another week.

3. As the developing miso nears maturity, take a sample. Remove the pressing lid and tilt the container so the tamari runs to one side. Partially pull back the cloth and plastic sheet, and take a sample from about 2 inches under the surface with a spoon.

4. When assessing if the miso is ready, consider three factors—color, aroma, and taste. The color should be the same as described in Table 3.1. Its aroma should be slightly alcoholic and yeasty, but pleasant smelling. (A strong alcoholic smell usually indicates the mixture has overheated or needs to ferment more. If this is the case, allow the mixture to develop a little longer in a cooler environment.) Finally, when mature, the harsh, salty taste of unfermented miso should be mellowed, and a subtle sweetness should be apparent, particularly with short-term varieties. If any miso type is too salty or too light, ferment it a little longer. Occasionally a batch of miso may develop a sour taste. This indicates that too little salt was added, it was diluted by the addition of too much water, or it wasn't thoroughly mixed with the other ingredients. Sour miso should be discarded.

STORING MATURE MISO

1. When you have determined that your miso is mature, scrape off and discard the thin surface layer ($\frac{1}{4}$ to $\frac{1}{2}$ inch), which is likely to be slightly off in color and taste.

2. Transfer the miso into small containers (1- to 4-pound capacity is recommended). With the exception of metal or aluminum, any food-grade container is fine. Glass is best, but plastic and stainless steel are also acceptable.

3. Store the mature miso in the refrigerator to prevent it from fermenting further. Ideally, sweet miso should be used within nine months, while dark, long-term miso is best to use within eighteen months. After this time, the miso can still be used, but its overall taste and quality will be diminished.

4. To release miso's full flavor, purée it in a suribachi, mortar, or grinder before using

SATISFACTION GUARANTEED

Making miso, which has been revered for generations as a precious, healthful food and one of Japan's culinary treasures, is a surprisingly easy process that requires only a few ingredients and a minimal amount of preparation time. Putting up your own batch of miso is a "hands-on" involvement through which a well-deserved sense of satisfaction is guaranteed.

Once you've made your own miso for the first time, don't be surprised if you continue to create standard traditional brews as well as interesting variations. In addition to gaining an appreciation for the process itself, you'll also be able to recognize the sometimes subtle differences between various miso types, and learn to identify high-quality varieties. Finally, having miso on hand will allow you to prepare delicious, healthful dishes that you can feel good about eating and serving to family and friends.

Cooking
with
Miso

4. Cooking Guidelines

From sweet and creamy to dark and robust, an exciting range of misos is now available in natural foods stores. While typical Japanese misos are made exclusively from soybeans, usually with the addition of cultured rice or barley, innovative American companies have developed new miso varieties by replacing some or all of the soybeans with ingredients like black soybeans, chick peas, millet, and even corn. Delicious and versatile, miso can enhance everything from basic macrobiotic dishes to elaborate gourmet fare.

The complex savory flavor of miso is difficult for Westerners to describe. The natural fermentation of soybeans and grains produces a blend of flavorful amino acids that cannot be expressed by the four basic tastes: sweet, salty, sour, and bitter. The Japanese consider this intriguing flavor to be a fifth taste, which they call *umami*, the flavor of Japan. The different proportions of soybeans, grain, and salt used to make various types of miso result in a range of tastes, but all share this umami quality—a distinctive flavor that stimulates the appetite and is uniquely satisfying.

Before learning the principles of cooking with miso, first, it's important to know how to shop for this unique food. No matter which variety of miso you're buying, always check labels for the words *unpasteurized, organic,* and *traditionally made,* which usually indicate a manufacturer's commitment to quality. We highly recommend using unpasteurized miso for its superior flavor and health benefits. Miso that is sold unrefrigerated in sealed plastic bags is almost certainly pasteurized or has an added preservative such as alcohol. (An exception to this rule is very old, dry soybean miso, such as Hatcho miso, which is not very active and can be packaged unpasteurized in sealed packets.) Because they produce carbon dioxide, most unpasteurized misos would explode if sealed in plastic bags. Most varieties are packaged in screw-top glass jars or plastic tubs and are found in the refrigerated section.

Choosing organic miso and other soy products has become even more important in recent years because of the rapidly increasing production of genetically modified soybeans. The issue of including genetically modified organisms (GMOs) in our food is a health concern that is garnering a great deal of attention in many countries. Since there are no federal laws regulating the labeling of products made with genetically modified ingredients, the only way to ensure that the miso you buy has not been made with genetically modified soybeans is to use miso that is made with organic ingredients. The guidelines for organic standards prohibit the use of GMOs. Therefore, when shopping for miso, be sure to check the ingredient list for organic soybeans.

The color of miso is another indication of its quality. Long-aged salty miso, marketed under such names as "brown rice miso," "barley miso," "red miso," and "rice miso" should be a rich russet or earthy brown color, not black or nearly black. I generally refer to these miso types as *dark* or *dark salty miso*. Sweet misos, which are marketed as "mellow white miso," "mellow barley miso," "white miso," "chickpea miso," and "sweet white miso" should be light in color, never brown. I refer to them collectively as *sweet miso.*

The key to fine miso cooking is to integrate the more subtle aspects of miso's color and flavor in a gentle balance with other ingredients, not to overpower dishes with its strong taste. For example, when making miso soup, using a kombu, shiitake, kombu-bonito, or vegetable stock as a base helps achieve a full, rich flavor with considerably less miso than you would need if you boiled vegetables in plain water and relied on miso to supply all the flavor. The latter method may result in either an overly salty soup or one that is watery and bland.

Light soups made with sweet miso tend to be more appealing during warm weather months. Bright summer vegetables, such as sweet corn and yellow squash, and lightly cooked greens are perfect eye-appealing additions to sweet miso's beautiful golden broth. During colder months, dark miso soup with its hearty flavor is the more popular choice. Chunky root vegetables, kale, and wakame are suitable ingredients for the earthy-colored dark miso broth.

Although miso will keep indefinitely in the refrigerator, it is best to use sweet miso within nine months and dark miso within eighteen months. Although you can still use the miso if stored longer, its flavor and quality will be diminished.

SWEET MISO

Certain general rules can be applied when cooking with light sweet misos as opposed to dark salty ones. The light color, sweet taste, and creamy texture of sweet miso is suggestive of its use in American-style cooking: it is an excellent dairy substitute. Instead of adding milk, butter, and salt to mashed potatoes or creamed soups, try a little sweet miso. Replace the sour cream typically used in dips and spreads, with a mixture of sweet miso, tofu, and lemon or rice vinegar.

To realize the full potential of sweet miso, explore its uses in salad dressings and sauces. Together, sweet miso and naturally brewed rice vinegar create a delicious tartness that is both refreshing and cooling. Known as *su miso*, this combination has a long history in Japanese cuisine. Blended with other ingredients, such as oil, onion, dill, rice syrup, tofu, and tahini, sweet miso and rice vinegar complement each other perfectly in American style dressings, dips, and sauces.

When combined with equal amounts of mirin or sake, sweet miso makes a delicious and versatile sauce for baked, broiled, or stir-fried vegetables, fish, and tofu. (Bringing it to a simmer, at least momentarily, evaporates the alcohol.) Add some to your favorite stir-fry during the last minute or two of cooking. Or combine it with sautéed slivered almonds for a wonderful amandine sauce—perfect over French-style green beans.

Create another versatile sauce by combining sweet miso with tahini that has been thinned with water or stock. Adding ingredients such as lemon, ginger, garlic, onion, mirin, and flavorful herbs changes the personality of this simple sauce to accompany a variety of dishes, particularly steamed or boiled vegetables, grains, noodles, and tofu. Substituting freshly roasted ground sesame seeds, pecans, or walnuts for the tahini achieves an especially delicious result.

DARK MISO

Dark salty misos combine nicely with beans, gravies, baked dishes, and hearty vegetable stews and soups. Try dark miso in thick soups that include root vegetables such as burdock, carrots, and daikon. A lentil casserole seasoned with dark miso warms the body and supplies plenty of high-quality protein. Although dark misos are not as versatile as sweet varieties, traditionally made, unpasteurized dark miso makes nutritious, flavorful and satisfying miso soups that you can enjoy every day in fall or winter without ever tiring of them.

Once the weather becomes warm, we prefer to combine a dark miso with a sweet variety when making soup. When mixed with sweet, tangy, or pungent ingredients, such as mirin, rice syrup, rice vinegar, or fresh ginger, dark miso adds refreshing flavor to sauces. Keep in mind, however, that dark miso is stronger in taste than sweet miso, so use it sparingly.

GENERAL QUALITIES

Both types of miso—dark and sweet—are suitable for certain special uses. In general, miso is a good choice when you are looking for a salting agent, pickling medium, digestive aid, or food tenderizer.

As a salting agent, miso supplies much more in terms of flavor and nutrition than plain salt, and without the harshness. When substituting miso for salt, add approximately one level tablespoon of any light, sweet miso or two level teaspoons of dark, salty miso for one-quarter teaspoon salt.

Miso is also an excellent pickling agent. Miso pickles (pickled vegetables) are nutritious, aid digestion, are easily prepared, and can be ready to eat in one to three days. Though any type of miso can be used, combining a dark and light miso offers particularly good results. Simply put a thin layer of miso in the bottom of a nonmetal container, add a layer of vegetables, then cover with more miso. No weight or pressing is necessary, but the container should be covered with a towel or sushi mat. Thin vegetables with a lot of surface area, such as cabbage leaves, can be pickled in one day. Large or dense vegetables should be quartered or sliced and may take two to three days. Always rinse the pickled vegetables before serving.

The powerful enzymatic action of unpasteurized miso is a natural digestive aid and tenderizing agent. In the digestive system, the enzymes present in miso aid the body's own resources in breaking down complex food molecules. Foods such as beans, raw tofu, and tomato products may cause digestive discomfort. Miso helps balance these foods, aiding in their digestion.

For the same reason miso aids digestion, it is also a great natural tenderizer. When used in marinades, it helps break down the complex molecules of vegetable fiber, animal protein, and fats into more readily digestible forms. At the same time, its flavor permeates the marinating foods.

Both sweet and dark misos can be used in place of stock. Instead of using beef, chicken, or fish stock in soups and sauces, we often use miso broth. We substitute sweet miso broth for chicken or fish stock, and dark miso broth for beef stock. Add 3 to 4 tablespoons of white miso or 2 to 3 tablespoons of dark miso to a quart of vegetable stock or water. (Of course, you can add more miso if desired.) When stir-frying, try adding a little miso mixed with white wine toward the end of the cooking time. This will help deglaze the pan and add moisture and rich flavor to the ingredients.

ADDING MISO TO FOODS

Although there are some exceptions, unpasteurized miso should be added to dishes at or near the end of cooking time. When making most soups or stews, for example, we add the miso at the last minute in order to preserve its full, fresh flavor as well as its beneficial enzymes and other microorganisms. However, when making a sauce or stew that is thickened with arrowroot or kuzu, both of which are usually added near the end of cooking, incorporate the miso first and allow it to simmer at least several minutes before adding the thickener. If miso is added along with or after the thickener, its enzymes will begin "digesting" the long carbohydrate chains that are needed to maintain thickness. The sauce or stew will then mysteriously revert to a liquid state. Although thoroughly cooking the miso will destroy its enzymes, other health benefits will be preserved.

It is best to mix the miso with some stock or other liquid before adding it to a recipe. This allows the miso to permeate the soup, stew, or sauce more evenly. When adding miso to soups, for example, simply ladle some of the hot broth over the miso in a small bowl, stir to dissolve, and then return the mixture to the pot. When incorporating miso into a thick mixture such as a tofu-based dip, first combine it with vinegar, lemon juice, or other liquid from the recipe. If the liquids have already been added, simply thin the miso in an equal amount of water.

BRIDGING THE GAP

For those with a commitment to healthful eating, cooking for family members or guests who are not accustomed to this eating style can be a challenge. Miso helps bridge this gap, bringing depth of flavor and a satisfying complexity to simple fare.

In some of the recipes in this book, we have specifically called for a particular miso. However, for any recipe that calls for simply a dark miso, any dark miso will do. This rule is generally true of sweet misos, as well; however, sweet varieties contain a greater range of salt. This means, depending on the specific sweet miso you are using, you may have to adjust the amount used to achieve the best results. Always taste the dish before serving.

ENJOY THE EXPERIENCE

The following chapters offer a wealth of miso recipes from appetizers to entrées. You will find some traditional Japanese dishes as well as dozens of recipes that use miso to enhance Western-style fare. It's easy to incorporate miso into your diet, and by doing so, you'll be adding rich flavor, nutrition, and health benefits. So it's time to get started! After trying a few of the following recipes, don't be surprised if you find yourself thinking of ways to add miso to many more of your culinary favorites. Enjoy the experience.

5. Dips and Spreads

Nutritious and easy to prepare, nut-, bean-, and tofu-based spreads and dips are wonderfully versatile bases for a variety of appetizing sandwiches and hors d'oeuvres. Preparing them with miso adds flavor, body, and nutrition. If you already have some favorite recipes of your own, try preparing them with miso instead of salt. Generally, we prefer to use sweet or mellow misos in most dips and spreads, but for certain bean-based recipes, hearty red, brown rice, or barley misos are better choices.

When preparing sandwiches or other finger foods, choose the bread or other "container" to suit the filling. A delicate filling, such as Tofu Salad Spread (page 45), goes best with thin, light breads, while thicker, heartier fillings, like Salmon Salad Spread (page 48) and Azuki Spread (page 52), are better suited on firmer, heavier breads, especially for open-faced sandwiches. The convenient pocket of a whole wheat pita is perfect for holding loose or difficult-to-manage fillings, such as seafood and tempeh salads. And don't forget about taco shells, chapattis and tortillas, which are no longer enjoyed only with their traditional ethnic fare. You can pair them with all kinds of spreads and fillings, like Sesame-Miso Spread (page 49) and Pinto Bean Spread (page 53).

Many of the recipes in this chapter are also great in tasty appetizers and hors d'oeuvres. You'll find old standbys like Hummus (page 51), as well as some unusual dips and spreads, like Red Lentil Paté (page 50) and Walnut-Miso Dip (page 51). All lend themselves to a myriad of simple, creative presentations. Enjoy them as flavorful dips for fresh vegetables and chips; delicious fillings for tea sandwiches, celery "boats," and croustades; or as savory spreads on your favorite crackers, breads, and rice cakes.

The majority of the following recipes are quick and easy to prepare. As an added bonus, most can be stored for at least three days in the refrigerator. You'll enjoy making them as well as serving them to family and friends.

Tofu "Cheese" and Olive Spread

Yield: About 1½ cups

8 ounces fresh tofu

2 tablespoons sweet or
   mellow miso (any type)

1 tablespoon tahini

¼ cup minced red onion

2 tablespoons mayonnaise or
   tofu mayonnaise

2 tablespoons chopped black
   or green olives

1 tablespoon plus
   1 teaspoon brown rice
   vinegar or lemon juice

1 clove garlic, finely minced

Several sprigs fresh dill,
   finely chopped, or ¼ cup
   chopped parsley

This tasty and nutritious spread is simple to prepare. Enjoy a generous layer on bread or crackers or in pita. Top with some lettuce, spinach, or sprouts.

1. Bring about 2 inches of water to a boil in a 2- or 3-quart saucepan, and gently slide the tofu into the boiling water (there should be enough water to cover the tofu). When the water returns to a boil, turn off the heat and cover the pot. Let sit for 3 to 5 minutes.

2. Drain the hot water from the pot and cover the tofu with cold water, allowing it to sit for several minutes to cool.

3. Remove the cooled tofu and wrap it in cheesecloth, muslin, or a clean kitchen towel. Gently squeeze out the excess water.

4. Place the tofu, miso and tahini in a medium bowl, and mash thoroughly. Mix in the remaining ingredients.

5. Use immediately, or place in the refrigerator for at least 30 minutes for heightened flavor. Refrigerated in a covered container, the spread will keep for about four days.

Tofu Salad Spread

By adding your own choice of fresh herbs or vegetables, such as minced celery or grated carrots, you can create many variations of this nutritious protein-rich spread.

1. Bring about 2 inches of water to a boil in a 2- or 3-quart saucepan, and gently slide the tofu into the boiling water (there should be enough water to cover the tofu). When the water returns to a boil, turn off the heat and cover the pot. Let sit for 3 to 5 minutes.

2. Drain the hot water from the pot and cover the tofu with cold water, allowing it to sit for several minutes to cool.

3. Remove the cooled tofu and wrap it in cheesecloth, muslin, or a clean kitchen towel. Gently squeeze out the excess water.

4. Place the tofu, miso and tahini in a medium bowl, and mash thoroughly. Mix in the remaining ingredients.

5. Use immediately, or place in the refrigerator for at least 30 minutes for heightened flavor. Refrigerated in a covered container, the spread will keep for about three days.

Yield: About 3 cups

1 pound fresh tofu

3 tablespoons sweet or mellow miso (any type)

3 tablespoons tahini, or ground toasted sesame seeds

$1/3$ cup minced scallions

$1/4$ cup minced parsley

2 cloves garlic, pressed or finely minced

$1^1/_2$–2 tablespoons brown rice vinegar or lemon juice

1 tablespoon unrefined light sesame or canola oil

$3/4$–1 teaspoon prepared mustard (optional)

Savory Miso- Sunflower Spread

Yield: About 3 cups

$^1/_2$ cup hulled sunflower seeds

2 tablespoons lemon juice or rice vinegar

2 tablespoons rice syrup

2 cloves garlic, minced

2 tablespoons chopped onion

$^1/_8$–$^1/_4$ cup water

3 tablespoons red, brown rice, or barley miso

1 tablespoon tahini

1 pound fresh tofu

Roasted sunflower seeds give this spread its wonderfully unique flavor.

1. In an unoiled, medium-sized skillet, roast the sunflower seeds over medium heat, stirring constantly for about 5 minutes, or until they are golden brown and fragrant.

2. Place the roasted seeds in a blender and chop to a fairly fine meal.

3. Add the lemon juice, rice syrup, garlic, onion, and enough water to blend the ingredients until thick but not crumbly.

4. Add the miso and tahini and continue to blend for about 10 seconds.

5. Crumble the tofu into the blender, and blend for about 30 seconds, or until smooth. If the mixture is too thick, add just a *little* more water as needed. Too much water will turn this spread into a dip!

6. Use immediately, or place in the refrigerator for at least 30 minutes for heightened flavor. Refrigerated in a covered container, the spread will keep for about three days.

Tempeh Salad Spread

*Adapted from a recipe in **The Book of Tempeh** by William Shurtleff and Akiko Aoyagi, this piquant tempeh spread tastes surprisingly like tuna salad. Sandwiched between slices of whole grain bread and topped with lettuce, watercress, sprouts, and slivered red onion, it's one of our family favorites.*

1. Place the tempeh in a steamer basket or on a steamer rack set over boiling water. Cover and steam for about 20 minutes.

2. Transfer the tempeh to a medium bowl. Immediately add the water and mash thoroughly while the tempeh is still hot. Allow to cool to room temperature.

3. Add the remaining ingredients to the tempeh and mix well.

4. Use immediately, or place in the refrigerator for at least 30 minutes for heightened flavor. Refrigerated in a covered container, the spread will keep for about four to five days.

Yield: About 2 cups

8 ounces tempeh, diced

1 1/2 tablespoons water

1/3 cup mayonnaise or tofu mayonnaise

2 tablespoons finely minced onion

2 tablespoons minced parsley

2 tablespoons fresh dill

1 tablespoon sweet or mellow miso mixed with 1 tablespoon water

2 teaspoons prepared mustard

Tulip Croustades

These crisp containers are the perfect vehicles for your favorite spreads. The following recipe makes a dozen croustades. They can be made a day ahead of time and stored in an airtight container before filling. And don't forget to garnish!

Remove the crusts from 12 slices of fresh bread, then flatten each slice with a rolling pin. Lightly brush both sides with a little vegetable oil, and then gently press the slices into a muffin tin. Bake in a preheated 350°F oven for about 20 minutes, or until golden in color. Allow to cool before filling. If made ahead of time, and humidity has caused them to lose their crispness, simply heat them in a 300°F oven for 10 minutes.

Salmon Salad Spread

Yield: About 2 cups

8 ounces cooked salmon

1 small ear corn, cooked (optional)

1 rib celery, finely minced

1–2 scallions, slivered

2 tablespoons chopped fresh dill, or 3 tablespoons minced watercress or parsley

Pinch white or black pepper (optional)

DRESSING

2 tablespoons extra-virgin olive oil

2 tablespoons lemon juice

2 teaspoons sweet or mellow white miso

Another family favorite. We sometimes use Creamy Ginger-Dill Dressing (page 62) instead of the one below.

1. Remove and discard the skin and any bones from the salmon. Flake the fish into a small bowl (using your hands to do this will help you notice any remaining bones).

2. If using corn, cut the kernels from the cob and toss them into the bowl with the salmon. Add the celery, scallions, dill, and pepper, if desired.

3. To make the dressing, whisk together the oil, lemon juice, and miso. Pour over the salmon mixture and toss until well combined. Use immediately.

4. Refrigerated in a covered container, this spread will keep for five to six days.

Tea Sandwiches

Most of the spreads in this chapter can be used in delicious and attractive tea sandwiches or canapés. These delightful appetizers are both fun to make and easy to prepare.

Remove the crusts from slices of fresh whole grain bread, then cut the slices into rectangles or triangles. Top with a generous layer of spread, and either cover with another piece of bread or serve open-faced with a garnish—sliced olives, pickles, cherry tomatoes, as well as sprigs of parsley, watercress, and dill are good choices. Be creative! You can also make three-layered canapés, using a light and dark bread with two complementary fillings. Arrange on a decorative platter and serve.

Instant Miso-Tahini Spread

A little of this tasty spread on a rice cake or cracker makes an instant snack or "appetizer" for hungry children who can't wait for dinner. Because it's so easy to make and tastes best when fresh, we recommend preparing only a little at a time.

1. In a small bowl, thoroughly combine the tahini, miso, and lemon juice. Mix in 1 tablespoon of water at a time until mixture is thick and spreadable. Use immediately.

2. Refrigerated in a covered container, this spread will keep for about a week.

Yield: About ½ cup

3 tablespoons tahini

1 tablespoon sweet or mellow miso

1 tablespoon lemon juice

3 tablespoons water (approximately)

Sesame-Miso Spread

This simple and tasty spread goes especially well on bread or toast, rice cakes, crackers, and chapatti. Although it keeps in the refrigerator for about a week, this spread is best when fresh, so we recommend preparing small amounts at a time.

1. Place all of the ingredients in a small saucepan or skillet and mix together well. Bring to a slow simmer over medium-low heat, stirring constantly. Continue to simmer gently for 1 to 2 minutes while stirring. The mixture should be somewhat thick but smooth. Remove from the heat.

2. The spread will continue to thicken as it cools. If too thick, stir in more water, a teaspoon at a time. Use immediately

3. Refrigerated in a covered container, this spread will keep for about a week.

Yield: About ½ cup

¼ cup tahini

¼ cup water

1 tablespoon red, brown rice, or barley miso, or 2 tablespoons sweet or mellow miso

2 tablespoons minced onion, scallion, or chives (optional)

1 teaspoon chopped fresh basil, or ¼ teaspoon dried (optional)

Red Lentil Paté

Yield: About 2¹/₂ cups

1 cup dried red lentils

3 cups water

¹/₂ teaspoon sea salt

2 tablespoons extra-virgin olive oil

¹/₂ cup minced onion or scallion

2–3 cloves garlic, minced

¹/₂ teaspoon dried marjoram

Pinch white pepper

3 tablespoons chopped parsley

1 tablespoon chopped fresh basil

1 tablespoon lemon juice

2 teaspoons red, brown rice, or barley miso mixed with 2 teaspoons water

Try this simple, golden-colored paté as a filling for small tarts, green pepper quarters, and celery boats, or as a tasty spread on your favorite crackers. When topped with slivered red onion, lettuce, and sprouts, it's also a satisfying sandwich filling.

1. Rinse the lentils with cold water, drain, and place in a 3-quart pot. Add the water and bring to a boil over high heat. Reduce the heat to medium-low, cover, and simmer the lentils for 25 to 30 minutes, or until tender.

2. Stir in the salt, and simmer uncovered 10 minutes more, or until most of the liquid has been absorbed. Remove from heat, mash the lentils, and set aside.

3. In a small skillet, heat 1 tablespoon of the oil over medium heat. Add the onion and garlic, and sauté for 2 to 3 minutes, or until the onion is soft and translucent. Add the marjoram and pepper, and continue to sauté a minute more.

4. Add the onion mixture to the lentils, along with the parsley, basil, lemon juice, miso, and remaining tablespoon of oil. Mix together well, and set aside to cool to room temperature before serving. The paté will thicken as it cools.

5. Refrigerated in a covered container, the paté will keep for about four days.

Stuffed Endive Hors D'Oeuvres

Here's an idea for a simple but elegant hors d'oeuvre.

Add a ¹/₂ cup of minced red bell pepper and a ¹/₂ cup of minced celery to 1¹/₂ cups of Creamy Dill Dip (page 54). Place rounded tablespoons of the mixture on the lower third of about 20 crisp Belgian endive leaves. Tuck a sprig of watercress or parsley into the dip so it rests on the leaf. Arrange the filled leaves on a platter in a fan-shaped pattern.

Hummus

This favorite Middle-Eastern dip is protein-rich and garlicky good!

1. Place all of the ingredients in a blender or food processor, and purée until thick and very smooth. If too thick, add a little more water to achieve the desired consistency.

2. Use immediately, or place in the refrigerator for at least 1 hour for heightened flavor.

3. Refrigerated in a covered container, the hummus will keep for about four to five days.

Yield: About 1³/₄ cups

1¹/₂ cups cooked chick peas

¹/₄ cup water

2 cloves garlic, minced

3 tablespoons tahini

2 tablespoons sweet or mellow miso

1¹/₂ tablespoons lemon juice

1 tablespoon extra-virgin olive oil

Walnut–Miso Dip

Serve this rich savory dip in a small bowl garnished with a walnut half and sprig of parsley.

1. In an unoiled medium-sized skillet, roast the walnuts over medium heat, stirring constantly for 5 to 7 minutes, or until golden brown and fragrant.

2. Place the roasted walnuts in a blender along with the miso and stock, and blend until smooth. If desired, add rice syrup to taste. Use immediately

3. Refrigerated in a covered container, the dip will keep for about two to three days.

Yield: About 1¹/₂ cups

1 cup walnuts*

3 tablespoons sweet or mellow miso

³/₄ cup vegetable stock or water

1–2 teaspoons rice syrup or mirin (optional)

*Pecans can be substituted for the walnuts.

Azuki Spread

Yield: About 2¹/₂ cups

1 cup dried azuki beans

3 cups water

¹/₄ teaspoon sea salt

1 tablespoon extra-virgin
   olive oil

1 medium onion, diced

2–3 cloves garlic, minced

¹/₄ teaspoon shoyu or tamari

2 teaspoons red, brown rice,
   or barley miso

1 tablespoon lemon juice

3 tablespoons minced parsley

Azuki beans have long been highly regarded in Japan for their rich nutritional and strengthening qualities. They are a good source of vitamins, minerals, and protein, and they are easier to digest than most beans. Although soaking reduces their cooking time, it isn't necessary. In addition to being a delicious spread for sandwiches and crackers, this recipe makes a wonderful mild filling for Mexican favorites like tacos and burritos.

1. Rinse the beans with cold water, drain, and place in a 3-quart pot. Add the water and bring to a boil over high heat. Reduce the heat to medium-low, cover, and simmer for 1¹/₂ hours, or until the azukis are tender. Add more water if needed.

2. Stir in the salt, and simmer uncovered 15 to 20 minutes more. Drain the beans, reserving any cooking liquid, and set aside.

3. In a medium skillet, heat the oil over medium heat. Add the onion and garlic, and sauté 3 to 5 minutes, or until soft and thoroughly cooked, but not browned.

4. Add the drained beans and sauté another 2 to 3 minutes, then stir in the shoyu and ¹/₃ cup of the reserved broth. While stirring, partially mash the beans.

5. Combine the miso and lemon juice, and add it to the bean mixture. If the spread is too dry, add a little more broth. Add the parsley and cook another minute.

6. Use immediately or allow to cool to room temperature. Refrigerated in a covered container, the spread will keep for about five days.

VARIATION

For a spicier taste, add 1 to 2 teaspoons of cumin to the sautéing onions and garlic.

Pinto Bean Spread

Next time you make tacos, try this tasty bean spread as a filling and add your favorite toppings. Minced sweet onion, chopped avocado, salsa, sliced olives, grated soy cheese, shredded lettuce, and sprouts are perfect choices.

1. Soak the beans in a quart of water for 8 to 12 hours.

2. Drain the beans and place in a 4-quart pot. Add the kombu and water, and bring to a boil over high heat. Reduce the heat to medium-low, cover loosely, and simmer for 2 hours, or until the beans are tender. Add the salt and bay leaf, and continue to simmer.

3. As the beans simmer, heat the oil in a medium skillet over medium heat. Add the onion, garlic, and green pepper, and sauté about 5 minutes, or until the onion is soft and translucent. Add the cumin, chili powder, and oregano, and continue to sauté for 1 to 2 minutes.

4. Add a ladle of the bean cooking liquid to the skillet, stir briefly, and then add the onion-green pepper mixture to the beans. Continue to cook, uncovered, for 15 to 20 minutes, or until the mixture is thick and moist, not dry. Add the parsley and miso during the last minute of cooking time.

5. Use immediately or allow to cool to room temperature.

6. Refrigerated in a covered container, the spread will keep for about five days.

Yield: About 2$\frac{1}{2}$ cups

1 cup pinto beans

6-inch strip kombu

3$\frac{1}{2}$ cups water

$\frac{3}{4}$ teaspoon sea salt

1 bay leaf

1 tablespoon extra-virgin olive oil

1 onion, minced

2 cloves garlic, finely minced

$\frac{1}{3}$ cup minced green bell pepper

1 teaspoon cumin

1 teaspoon chili powder (or to taste)

$\frac{1}{2}$ teaspoon oregano

2 tablespoons chopped parsley or cilantro

1 tablespoon red, brown rice, or barley miso mixed with 1 tablespoon water

Creamy Dill Dip

Yield: 1½ cups

8 ounces fresh tofu

¼ cup sweet or mellow miso

2 tablespoons brown rice
   vinegar or lemon juice

2 tablespoons light sesame
   or canola oil

1 or 2 cloves garlic, chopped

Several sprigs fresh dill,
   chopped

Popular with any crowd and a breeze to prepare, this versatile dip is one of our first choices when planning a party.

1. Bring about 2 inches of water to a boil in a 2- or 3-quart saucepan, and gently slide the tofu into the boiling water (there should be enough water to cover the tofu). When the water returns to a boil, turn off the heat and cover the pot. Let sit for 3 to 5 minutes.

2. Drain the hot water from the pot and cover the tofu with cold water, allowing it to sit for several minutes to cool.

3. Remove the cooled tofu and wrap it in cheesecloth, muslin, or a clean kitchen towel. Gently squeeze out the excess water.

4. Crumble the tofu into a blender, add the remaining ingredients, and blend until smooth. If the mixture is too thick to blend, add a little water, rice milk, or soy milk.

5. Place the mixture in a bowl, cover, and refrigerate for at least 2 hours. Adjust the seasonings before using.

6. Refrigerated in a covered container, the spread will keep about four days.

VARIATION

For a creamy onion dip, use 3 tablespoons minced fresh onion or 2 tablespoons dried instead of the dill. Add the onion after the other ingredients have been blended together.

6. The Salad Bowl

There once was a time when "salad" meant little more than a bowl of iceberg lettuce, tomato, and cucumber. Fortunately, a growing emphasis on health and nutrition has changed that image. From being an uninspired course, the salad has evolved into one of the most varied, nutritious, and stimulating parts of a meal. It can serve as a light prelude to the main course, the entrée itself, or a palate-cleansing finale. Today's salads are creative affairs that can include everything from legumes and whole grains to fruits and vegetables—from both land and sea. Along with adding flavor, texture, and interest to an otherwise boring dish, many of these salad additions are nutritional powerhouses and mainstays of the natural foods diet.

Salad dressings, which once had to be high in fat to be delicious, have come a long way, too. They tend to call for small measures of high-quality oils in combination with premium vinegars and fresh herbs—lower in fat, yet big on flavor. Salad dressings are also excellent for incorporating beneficial essential fatty acids (EFAs) into your diet. Linoleic acid (omega-6 fatty acid) and linolenic acid (omega-3 fatty acid) are essential to health. They cannot be produced synthetically, so they must be present in the diet in sufficient amounts. Unrefined vegetables oils are a good source of these EFAs, which are necessary for many important body functions,

including energy production, regulation of various cell functions, growth, hemoglobin production, and immune system response.

It is important to maintain a good balance of linoleic and linolenic acids; but this is difficult because linoleic acid is much more prevalent in a wider variety of foods. Since flax oil has an abundance of linolenic acid and a delicious, nutty flavor, we recommend substituting flax oil for half of the oil in most salad dressing recipes. Since flax oil should not be heated, don't use it in dressings that are warm or hot, such as Hot Miso Dressing (page 61). It must be refrigerated and should be used within six months.

Many unrefined vegetable oils are also rich in vitamin E, the body's primary fat-soluble antioxidant. Vitamin E protects cell membranes and other fatty areas of the body, including the brain. Its proven benefits are well documented.

Miso's use as a flavor enhancer in salad dressings lends even greater health and nutritional benefits. In general, sweet and mellow misos are the most suitable varieties and can be substituted for the salt in almost any recipe. One tablespoon of sweet or mellow miso is equivalent to approximately one-quarter teaspoon salt.

Most of the dressings in this chapter are low in fat and easy to make. Some are variations of traditional favorites, while others are more innovative, making use of ingredients found in a natural foods pantry. You'll find the fresh taste of homemade dressings immeasurably better than commercial varieties, and because you make them yourself, you can control the proportion and quality of the ingredients.

In addition to including a wide variety of dressings, this chapter also presents some of our favorite salad recipes. Just keep in mind that almost any healthful food can be tossed into the salad bowl to create wonderful variations in short order. To stimulate the appetite, try a simple duo of tender bibb lettuce and slivered red onion topped with Coconut-Lime Dressing (page 64). During the winter, when fresh local greens may be in short supply, try the Arame Salad (page 71), a light, mineral-rich sea vegetable salad that is the perfect accompaniment to hearty winter entrées. When the temperature soars, add protein-rich marinated beans, golden fried tofu, or seasoned tempeh to make any salad a main event. The possibilities are endless, limited only by your imagination.

SALAD DRESSINGS

Tahini-Herb Dressing

This dressing, which goes well with most tossed or pasta salads, offers plenty of flavor and a creamy texture without any oil. The parsley and chives add a spark of color and fresh taste.

1. Place the water, tahini, miso, rice vinegar, cider vinegar, and garlic in a small bowl and stir until well mixed. If necessary, add more water to reach desired consistency. Stir in the parsley and chives, and transfer to a jar with a lid.

2. Use immediately, or cover and chill until ready to use. Shake well before using.

Yield: About 1 cup

$1/3$ cup water

$1/4$ cup toasted or raw tahini

2 tablespoons sweet or mellow miso

2 tablespoons brown rice vinegar or lemon juice

$1/2$ teaspoon apple cider vinegar

1 small clove garlic, pressed or minced

$1 1/2$ tablespoons minced fresh parsley

1 tablespoon fresh chopped chives or 1 teaspoon dried

Lemon-Tahini Dressing

This simple dressing goes well with salads featuring flavor-intense vegetables or greens such as watercress. Try it with Dulse-Watercress Salad (page 70).

1. Place the tahini, lemon juice, and miso in a small bowl or suribachi and combine well. Mix in water, 1 tablespoon at a time, until the desired consistency is achieved.

2. Use immediately, or cover and chill until ready to use.

Yield: About $1/3$ cup

2 tablespoons tahini

1 tablespoon lemon juice

1 tablespoon sweet or mellow miso

Water to desired consistency

Sesame-Tofu Dressing

Yield: About 1²/₃ cups

1 tablespoon sesame seeds

¹/₃ pound fresh silken or firm tofu

¹/₄ cup safflower oil

¹/₄ cup water

3 tablespoons sweet or mellow miso

2¹/₂ tablespoons brown rice vinegar or apple cider vinegar

1 tablespoon rice syrup or mirin

2 teaspoons toasted sesame oil

1 clove garlic, sliced

This delicious creamy dressing is considerably lower in fat than most French or Italian-style dressings.

1. In a small unoiled skillet, toast the sesame seeds over medium heat, stirring constantly, for 1 or 2 minutes, or until they are fragrant. Immediately transfer to a small bowl and set aside.

2. Place all of the ingredients except the sesame seeds in a blender. Blend until smooth, transfer to a jar with a lid, and stir in the sesame seeds.

3. Refrigerate before serving. Shake well before using.

Tofu Tips

☐ When shopping for tofu, freshness is key. Most tofu comes in a vacuum package with an expiration date. It is best to buy the tofu at least a week or two before this date. If purchasing bulk tofu, find out when it was delivered. Bulk tofu is not pasteurized, so it can be contaminated easily. It should be stored in the refrigerator, submerged in a tub of water that is changed daily.

☐ Fresh tofu should have a slightly sweet smell. A sour aroma indicates that it is beginning to spoil and should be discarded.

☐ Fresh tofu should be off-white in color and have a texture that is smooth but not slimy.

☐ Tofu that is prepackaged in water can be stored in the package in your refrigerator. However, once the package is open, the tofu should be submerged in a tub of water that is changed daily.

Creamy Herb Dressing

This creamy herb-flecked dressing is great on any tossed salad.

1. Place all of the ingredients in a blender and blend until smooth. If necessary, add more water or wine to reach desired consistency. Transfer to a jar with a lid.

2. Use immediately, or cover and chill until ready to use. Shake well before using.

Yield: About 2 cups

$1/3$ pound fresh silken or firm tofu

$1/2$ cup blush or semi-sweet white wine

$1/4$ cup safflower oil

$1/4$ cup firmly packed chopped parsley, or 3 tablespoons chopped dill leaves

3 tablespoons lemon juice or brown rice vinegar

2 tablespoons sweet or mellow miso

2 tablespoons water

1 tablespoon tahini

1 tablespoon rice syrup or mirin

1 small clove garlic, sliced

☐ If tofu looks and smells fine, but its freshness is questionable, before using it in salad dressings or other uncooked recipes, submerge it in a pot of boiling water, reduce the heat, and let it simmer for 2 or 3 minutes. Then transfer the tofu to a cold-water bath and let it sit until thoroughly cooled.

☐ Some recipes require pressing the tofu to remove excess water. For these recipes, start with firm or extra-firm tofu, which has a lower water content than soft or silken varieties. Cut the block into slices of even thickness. Spread a clean linen or cotton towel on a cutting board, arrange the slices on top, and cover with another cloth. Pat the tofu gently. Place a cookie sheet and a five-pound weight on top of the slices and let stand for 10 to 15 minutes. Raise one end of the sheet slightly to allow the water to drain. (When using extra-firm tofu, simply wrapping the slices in cloth and patting them may be sufficient for removing the water.)

Green Empress Dressing

Yield: About 3 cups

6 ounces fresh silken or firm tofu

1 ripe medium avocado, peeled and pitted

$1/3$ cup water

$1/4$ cup safflower or canola oil

$1/4$ cup sweet or mellow miso

$1/4$ cup minced fresh parsley

3 tablespoons brown rice vinegar or apple cider vinegar

2 tablespoons chopped onion

1 clove garlic, sliced

This recipe combines the nutritional goodness of avocado, tofu, and miso in a mild and creamy dressing.

1. Place all of the ingredients, but only half the parsley, in a blender and blend until smooth. If necessary, add more water to reach the desired consistency. Stir in the remaining parley, and transfer to a jar with a lid.

2. Use immediately, or cover and chill until ready to use. Shake well before using.

Lemon-Mint Dressing

Yield: About $1/4$ cup

1 tablespoon extra-virgin olive oil

2 teaspoons lemon juice

$1^1/2$ teaspoons sweet or mellow miso

$1/4$ teaspoon Dijon-style mustard

1 tablespoon plus 1 teaspoon minced fresh mint

The fresh, tantalizing taste of this simple dressing goes particularly well with parboiled vegetables, like green beans, zucchini, cauliflower, and carrots.

1. Combine the olive oil and lemon juice in a small bowl and stir until well blended. Add the miso and mustard, mix well, and then stir in the mint. Transfer to a jar with a lid.

2. Use immediately, or cover and chill until ready to use. Shake well before using.

Hot Miso Dressing

This dressing is simply delicious. We highly recommend it on Wilted Lettuce Salad (page 70) and Spinach Salad with Golden Fried Tofu (page 67)

Yield: About 1 cup

$1/_3$ cup water

$1/_4$ cup brown rice vinegar or red wine vinegar

1 tablespoon mellow white miso

3 tablespoons canola or safflower oil

$1/_2$ small onion, finely minced

Pinch dried basil

1. Place the water and vinegar in a small saucepan and bring to a boil. Remove from the heat, add the miso, and stir vigorously with a fork or whisk until dissolved. Transfer the mixture to a bowl and set aside.

2. Clean the pan, add the oil, and place over medium heat. Add the onion and sauté 1 or 2 minutes, or until soft and translucent. Add the basil and miso-vinegar mixture, increase the heat a bit, and bring to a boil while stirring.

3. Pour the hot dressing over the salad and serve.

Mustard Vinaigrette

This popular dressing enhances most tossed green salads. It's also great with salads that feature grains or parboiled vegetables.

Yield: About $2/_3$ cup

2–3 tablespoons brown rice vinegar or lemon juice

1 tablespoon sweet or mellow miso

1 tablespoon Dijon-style mustard

$1/_3$ cup extra-virgin olive oil

1. Place the vinegar, miso, and mustard in a small bowl and stir well. Add the oil and stir vigorously with a fork or whisk until well blended. Transfer to a jar with a lid.

2. Use immediately, or cover and chill until ready to use. Shake well before using.

Creamy Ginger-Dill Dressing

Yield: About 2½ cups

1 cup safflower oil

½ cup loosely packed chopped fresh dill

⅓ cup sweet or mellow miso

5 tablespoons brown rice vinegar

1 tablespoon mirin

1 tablespoon diced fresh ginger

1 shallot, peeled and chopped, or 2 tablespoons chopped onion

½ cup water

Fresh dill gives this thick creamy dressing its vibrant color; ginger gives it a fresh taste.

1. Place all of the ingredients except the water in a blender, and blend until smooth and thick. While the blender is running, remove the lid and add the water in a thin stream. If necessary, add more water to reach desired consistency. Transfer the dressing to a jar with a lid.

2. Refrigerate at least 2 hours before serving. As it chills, the dressing will thicken and its flavors will heighten. Shake well before using.

Oil and Vinegar Dressing

Yield: About 1 cup

⅔ cup extra-virgin olive oil

3–4 tablespoons red or white wine vinegar, or brown rice vinegar

1 small clove garlic, finely minced

2 tablespoons sweet or mellow miso

1 tablespoon minced fresh basil

1 tablespoon minced fresh parsley

1 teaspoon minced fresh oregano

½ teaspoon dry mustard (optional)

¼ teaspoon white or black pepper

Italian dressings are almost invariably a combination of olive oil and vinegar or lemon juice, often with salt, pepper, garlic, and herbs or spices added. The usual proportion is 1 part vinegar or lemon juice to 2 or 3 parts olive oil, depending on individual tastes and the sharpness of the vinegar. Miso replaces the salt in this recipe.

1. Place all of the ingredients in a small bowl and stir vigorously with a fork or whisk until well blended and smooth. Transfer to a jar with a lid.

2. Use immediately, or cover and chill until ready to use. Shake well before using.

Basil Vinaigrette

Basil lovers, this one's for you. A richly flavored relative of pesto, this dressing is perfect with most pasta salads and tossed salads. Try it with the Italian Bread Salad (page 68).

1. Place all of the ingredients in a blender or food processor, and blend until the basil is puréed and the dressing is smooth. Transfer to a jar with a lid.

2. Use immediately, or cover and chill until ready to use. Shake well before using.

Yield: About 1²/₃ cups

1 cup firmly packed fresh basil leaves

³/₄ cup extra-virgin olive oil

5 tablespoons red wine vinegar

1 small clove garlic, minced

2 tablespoons sweet or mellow white miso

1 tablespoon rice syrup or 1 teaspoon honey

¹/₄ teaspoon sea salt

¹/₈ teaspoon black or white pepper (optional)

Mellow Miso Dressing

Light, sweet misos make wonderful creamy salad dressings. We consider this one our "house dressing." Always popular with guests, it's the one we keep coming back to.

1. Place all of the ingredients in a blender and blend until smooth. If necessary, add more water to reach desired consistency. Transfer to a jar with a lid.

2. Use immediately, or cover and chill until ready to use. Shake well before using.

Yield: About 1 cup

¹/₃ cup safflower oil

¹/₄ cup water

3 tablespoons sweet or mellow miso

1¹/₂ tablespoons brown rice vinegar or apple cider vinegar

1 tablespoon chopped onion

2 teaspoons rice syrup or 1 tablespoon mirin

¹/₄–¹/₂ teaspoon dried mustard, or 2 tablespoons chopped fresh dill

Coconut-Lime Dressing

Yield: About ³/₄ cup

2 tablespoons fresh lime juice

2 tablespoons coconut milk

2 teaspoons maple syrup

1 tablespoon sweet or mellow miso

1 tablespoon water

¹/₄ cup canola oil

3 tablespoons shredded unsweetened coconut

Creamy coconut milk and tangy lime juice give this unique dressing a Caribbean flavor that can turn a summer salad into an exotic experience. Feel free to replace the maple syrup with honey or another sweetener.

1. Place the lime juice, coconut milk, maple syrup, miso, and water in a blender. With the blender running, remove the lid and add the oil in a thin stream. Blend until smooth, then stir in the shredded coconut. Transfer the dressing to a jar with a lid.

2. Use immediately, or cover and chill until ready to use. Shake well before using

"Miso Islands" Dressing

Yield: About 1²/₃ cups

1 cup mayonnaise or tofu mayonnaise

¹/₄ cup catsup

3 tablespoons sweet or mellow miso

1 tablespoon rice vinegar or apple cider vinegar

1 tablespoon rice syrup, or ¹/₂ tablespoon honey

1 tablespoon finely grated onion

1 tablespoon grated fresh horseradish

2 tablespoons relish (optional)

In addition to enjoying this flavorful "Thousand Island-style" dressing on tossed salads, be sure to try it on tofu or veggie burgers.

1. Place all of the ingredients in a small bowl and stir until well blended. Transfer to a jar with a lid.

2. Use immediately, or cover and chill until ready to use. Shake well before using.

Amazake Dressing

This slightly sweet yet tart dressing is terrific on grain, vegetable, and pasta salads.

1. Place all of the ingredients in a blender, and blend until smooth. Transfer to a jar with a lid.

2. Use immediately, or cover and chill until ready to serve. Shake well before using.

Yield: About 1 cup

$1/_2$ cup amazake

$1/_4$ cup brown rice vinegar

2 tablespoons light sesame oil

2 tablespoons extra-virgin olive oil

1 tablespoon red or brown rice miso

1 clove garlic, sliced

Creamy Basil-Mustard Dressing

The combination of mustard, wine vinegar, and lemon juice gives this creamy Italian-style dressing its zesty, stimulating taste. Try it on cooked vegetables as well as salads. Its pleasant green color will turn dark within a few days, so serve it fresh.

1. Place all of the ingredients except the olive oil and canola oil in a blender. With the blender running, remove the lid and add the oils in a thin stream. Blend until smooth. Transfer the dressing to a jar with a lid.

2. Use immediately, or cover and chill until ready to use. Shake well before using

Yield: About 1 cup

2 small cloves garlic

2 tablespoons chopped onion

2 tablespoons chopped fresh basil

2 tablespoons sweet or mellow miso

2 tablespoons water

1 tablespoon rice syrup

1 tablespoon white wine vinegar

1 tablespoon lemon juice

$1/_2$ teaspoon Dijon-style mustard

2 tablespoons extra-virgin olive oil

2 tablespoons canola oil

Cool-as-a-Cucumber Dressing

Yield: About 1½ cups

1 medium pickling cucumber

2 tablespoons chopped onion

2 tablespoons lemon juice

2 tablespoons sweet or mellow miso

2 tablespoons water

1 tablespoon rice syrup

1 tablespoon lemon zest

1 tablespoon chopped dill

1/8 teaspoon black pepper

1/4 cup walnut oil

This refreshing vinegar-free dressing adds plenty of zest to that midsummer salad. If you find the walnut oil too strong, use half walnut and half canola oil instead.

1. Place all of the ingredients except the oil in a blender. With the blender running, remove the lid and add the oil in a thin stream. Blend until smooth. Transfer the dressing to a jar with a lid.

2. Use immediately, or cover and chill until ready to use. Shake well before using

Brother Steve's Zesty Crimson Dressing

Yield: About ¾ cup

2 tablespoons sweet or mellow miso

2 tablespoons water

2 tablespoons brown rice vinegar

1 tablespoon brown rice syrup

1 tablespoon chopped red onion

1 tablespoon grated beet

2 teaspoons fresh ginger juice

1/4 cup canola oil

After his cholesterol medication failed to have much effect, John's brother Steve began drinking miso soup with shiitake mushrooms twice a day. Within a short time, his cholesterol levels dropped radically. Now Steve adds miso to everything. This brightly colored dressing, which is one of his creations, looks beautiful on salads with light-colored vegetables.

1. Place all of the ingredients except the oil in a blender. With the blender running, remove the lid and add the oil in a thin stream. Blend until smooth. Transfer the dressing to a jar with a lid.

2. Use immediately, or cover and chill until ready to use. Shake well before using.

SALAD CREATIONS

Spinach Salad with Golden Fried Tofu

Traditional spinach salads are garnished with hard boiled eggs and topped with hot bacon dressing. Our version uses golden cubes of fried tofu and tangy hot miso dressing instead.

1. Cut the tofu into ½-inch-thick slices and press to remove excess water (see guidelines on page 59). Cut into ½-inch cubes.

2. Place about 1 inch of oil in a small saucepan, place over medium-high heat, and heat to 350°F to 375°F.* Without crowding the pot, fry several tofu cubes at a time until lightly golden and crisp. Remove and drain on paper towels.

3. Divide the spinach among 4 individual salad bowls or plates, and top with tofu cubes. Drizzle the hot dressing over the salads and serve immediately.

Yield: 4 servings

8 ounces firm tofu

Safflower or canola oil for deep-frying

8 cups fresh spinach, stems removed

Hot Miso Dressing (page 61)

* If you don't have a deep-fry thermometer, place a wooden chopstick in the oil. When bubbles form around it, the oil is hot enough.

Mediterranean Salad

The long, hot Mediterranean summers have inspired an array of tempting salads, ranging from marinated vegetable and bean offerings to pasta and seafood creations. This flavorful tossed salad is one of our favorites.

1. Steam or parboil the cauliflower in lightly salted water for 2 to 3 minutes. Drain immediately and cool to room temperature.

2. Divide the greens among 4 individual salad bowls or plates. Top with onions, cauliflower, and olives. Add the dressing just before serving.

Yield: 4 servings

3 cups cauliflower florets

6 cups mixed salad greens

¼ red onion, thinly sliced

2 tablespoons sliced Kalamata olives

Oil and Vinegar Dressing (page 62)

Italian Bread Salad

Yield: 4 servings

8 cups bite-sized pieces
  Romaine lettuce, or salad
  greens of choice

3 cups day-old Italian, French,
  or sourdough bread cut into
  1-inch cubes

12 cherry tomatoes, halved

2 pickling cucumbers, halved
  lengthwise, then cut crosswise
  into $1/4$-inch slices

$1/4$ large red onion, very thinly
  sliced

Pinch sea salt

Basil Vinaigrette (page 63)

One of the traditional ways Italians use stale bread is in salads. Serve a large portion of this flavorful bread salad as a light but complete summer lunch, or enjoy it as a side dish along with an entrée. Any vinaigrette will work, but for a real Italian flair, we recommend Basil Vinaigrette.

1. Place all of the ingredients except the dressing in a large bowl and toss to mix.

2. Drizzle the dressing over the salad, and toss well. Let sit five minutes before serving.

Making Croutons

Croutons add a full-flavored crunch to salads, an appetizing spark to soups, and a crowning touch to casseroles. Either plain and unadorned or seasoned with your favorite herbs, these toasted bread cubes are quick and easy to make. And any type of bread will do—whole wheat, sourdough, rye, multi-grain, and raisin to name a few. As far as flavors, the sky's the limit—just about any combination of herbs and spices will do. (Be sure to try the Marjoram-Garlic Croutons on the next page.) If ever there was a garnish that encouraged creativity, croutons are it!

Marjoram-Garlic Croutons

Crisp and savory, these flavorful croutons are our favorite additions to most soups and salads.

1. Rub a heavy, medium-sized skillet with the cut sides of one or two pieces of garlic.

2. Add the oil to the skillet along with the garlic and place over medium-low heat. Sauté the garlic, stirring occasionally for 3 to 4 minutes or until just golden. Remove and discard the garlic. Stir in the marjoram and sauté 1 minute.

3. Add the bread cubes to the skillet and toss to coat. Increase the heat to medium and cook about 10 minutes, or until lightly toasted and crisp. Stir frequently to ensure even toasting.

4. Sprinkle with salt, toss, and transfer to paper towels to cool.

VARIATION

To bake the croutons, preheat the oven to 350°F. Substitute ¼ teaspoon garlic powder for the fresh, and combine it with the olive oil and marjoram in a bowl. Add the bread cubes and toss to coat evenly. Spread out the cubes in a single layer on an unoiled baking sheet. Bake for about 7 minutes, turn the croutons over, and bake 8 minutes more or until golden brown. Sprinkle with salt, toss, and allow to cool before using.

Yield: 1½ cups

2 large cloves garlic, quartered lengthwise

2 tablespoons extra-virgin olive oil

2 teaspoons crumbled dried marjoram

1½ cups whole wheat bread, cut into ½-inch cubes

Pinch sea salt

Wilted Lettuce Salad

Yield: 4 servings

4 cups bite-sized pieces bibb lettuce

4 cups bite-sized pieces Romaine lettuce

$^1/_4$ Vidalia onion or large red onion, very thinly sliced

$1^1/_2$ cups Marjoram-Garlic Croutons (page 69)

Hot Miso Dressing (page 61)

This is one of our family's favorite salads. We enjoy it all year long.

1. Divide the lettuce among 4 individual salad bowls or plates. Top with onions and croutons.

2. Drizzle the hot dressing over the salads. Serve immediately.

Dulse–Watercress Salad

Yield: 4 servings

$^1/_4$ cup dried dulse

$1^1/_2$ cups watercress

1 medium cucumber

6 cups bite-sized pieces bibb lettuce

2–3 radishes, thinly sliced

2 tablespoons toasted sunflower seeds

Lemon-Tahini Dressing (page 57)

An interesting combination of ingredients in this highly nutritious salad gives it a tantalizing, somewhat exotic taste.

1. Place the dulse in a bowl with enough lukewarm water to cover. Soak for 5 minutes or until just tender. Rinse carefully, drain well, and coarsely chop. Place in a medium-sized bowl. Peel, quarter, and slice the cucumber. Add it to the bowl along with the watercress. Toss well.

2. Divide the lettuce among 4 individual salad bowls or plates. Place mounds of the dulse mixture on top, arrange radish slices around the edge, and sprinkle with sunflower seeds. Add the dressing and serve.

Green Bean and Carrot Salad

This summer salad is enhanced by the refreshing flavors of lemon and mint.

1. In a steamer set over boiling water, steam the green beans and carrots for 3 minutes, or until crisp and colorful, but not raw. Transfer to a medium bowl along with the scallions.

2. Add the dressing, toss well, and serve.

Yield: 3 servings

2 cups French-cut green beans

1¼ cups julienned carrots

2 tablespoons slivered scallions

Lemon-Mint Dressing (page 60)

Arame Salad

This exotic sea vegetable salad is as eye appealing as it is delicious. The nearly black arame offers a dramatic visual contrast to the bed of lettuce it sits on. Creamy white tofu dressing provides even greater contrast.

1. Place the arame in a bowl with enough lukewarm water to cover. Soak for 5 to 10 minutes or until tender. Drain well and set aside.

2. Place the water, soy sauce, and mirin in a small saucepan and bring to a boil. Add the arame, reduce the heat to medium-low, and simmer for 25 minutes, or until the arame is tender. Drain well and cool to room temperature.

3. Divide the lettuce among 4 individual salad bowls or plates, and top with the arame. Add the dressing, garnish with parsley, and serve.

Yield: 4 servings

1 cup dry arame

5 cups water

1 tablespoon natural soy sauce

1 teaspoon mirin (optional)

6 cups lettuce leaves

Sesame-Tofu Dressing (page 58)

Minced parsley for garnish

Hearty Chef Salad

Yield: 4 servings

8 cups bite-sized pieces Romaine or bibb lettuce

8 ounces prepared tempeh "bacon"*

1$\frac{1}{2}$ cups coarsely chopped watercress or spinach

1 cucumber, peeled, quartered lengthwise, and sliced

1 small red onion, halved, and thinly sliced in half moons

1 medium carrot, shaved with a vegetable peeler

12 green or Kalamata olives, pitted and sliced

1 small yellow summer squash, thinly sliced

1 cup thinly sliced seitan strips

2–3 radishes, thinly sliced

Mustard Vinaigrette (page 61)

*Deep-fried tempeh and baked flavored tofu are other good choices.

When the temperature soars, make this salad the meal's main event.

1. Divide the lettuce among 4 individual dinner plates or wide shallow bowls.

2. Toss together the tempeh, watercress, cucumber, onion, carrot, and olives. Place mounds of the mixture on top of the lettuce leaves.

3. Alternate squash slices and strips of seitan around the edge of each mound. Arrange radish slices attractively on top of the mixture. Add the dressing and serve.

7. Soup for All Seasons

Few dishes can bring about a feeling of warmth and well-being like a good soup. A gently bubbling stockpot can fill the entire house with a tantalizing aroma that seems to have a power of its own. Whether a thick and hearty stew or a light, appetite-stimulating first course, homemade soups warm the heart and satisfy the soul.

Nourishing pots of broth brimming with the local bounty of land and sea have brought families together and sustained them throughout the ages. Along with its other attributes, soup's restorative powers have been praised around the world. People in United States tend to credit homemade chicken soup with having medicinal powers, but each culture has its own healthy favorite. In Japan, miso soup is revered for its health sustaining and restoring abilities. Recent scientific studies have uncovered what the Japanese have believed for centuries—miso is a concentrated source of nutrients as well as a potent medicine (see Chapter 2, "Miso Medicine"). It is for this reason that the Japanese add miso to soup, which they drink traditionally twice a day. Over the years, miso has extended beyond Japan, making its way into the diets of people throughout the world.

In addition to its use in time-honored Japanese-style soups, miso is a flavor enhancer for other soup varieties as well. When substituted for some or all of the salt in a recipe, miso supplies much more in terms of flavor and nutrition. Dark salty misos add a deep rich flavor and meaty quality to hearty soups, while the sweet taste and creamy texture of light-colored sweet misos makes them excellent substitutes for milk, butter, and salt in cream-style soups.

In general, miso is added to the simmering soup during the last minute or two of cooking. Although boiling does not significantly affect miso's nutritional profile or most of its medicinal qualities, it does destroy the beneficial microorganisms. Therefore, subjecting miso to prolonged high temperatures should be avoided when possible. However, in recipes like Creamy Celery Soup (page 92), in which a thickener is added at the end of cooking, the miso is boiled for several minutes. This is because the starch and protein-digesting enzymes in unpasteurized miso tend to counteract the effect of thickening agents.

This chapter begins with a variety of stock recipes that can be used as bases for many soups, sauces, and stews. It then presents a seasonal array of traditional Japanese-style miso soups. What follows next is a collection of some of our favorite "cream" soups and bean soups in which miso is used as a flavor enhancer. Many of these recipes, such as Grandma's Lentil Soup (page 97) and Vegetable Barley Stew (page 103) have been in our family for years, while other more contemporary creations, such as Caribbean Fish Chowder (page 101), Creamy Squash Soup with Coconut Milk (page 89), and Potato Leek Chowder with Roasted Garlic (page 87), were created with the help of John Belleme, Jr., chef extraordinaire and co-founder of Zemi, one of South Florida's finest restaurants.

Ranging from light first-course offerings to thick and hearty winter favorites, the majority of recipes in this chapter are economical, simple to prepare, and low in fat and calories. With an understanding of the basics of making stocks and soups, you can use the recipes in this chapter as springboards for creations of your own.

STOCKS

Kombu Stock

This subtle, flavor-enhancing Japanese stock is quick to prepare and requires only kombu and water. Kombu contains glutamic salts, the natural form of monosodium glutamate, which make this sea vegetable an excellent flavoring agent.

Yield: 6 cups

6-inch piece dried kombu

6 cups water

1. Place the kombu and water in a 3-quart pot. If time permits, let sit for 15 minutes before bringing to a boil over medium heat. Reduce the heat to medium-low and gently simmer, uncovered, for 2 to 3 minutes. Immediately remove the kombu and reserve for another use.

2. Use the stock immediately, refrigerate in a covered container for up to 5 days, or freeze for up to 6 months.

Stocks

The French call stocks *fonds de cuisine*—"foundations of cooking." Many successful soups, stews, and sauces begin with these bases. Aside from having more flavor than water, meatless stocks have other advantages. For starters, when preparing certain stocks, you can use leftover vegetables and trimmings that might otherwise go to waste. These ingredients add nutrients as well as flavor. As an added bonus, using a full-bodied stock allows you to rely less on salt or salty seasonings. Leftover stock can be stored in the refrigerator for a few days, or frozen for up to six months. Finally, stocks are simple to prepare (many can be made on the spur of the moment).

   If you're caught without a stock on hand and don't have the ingredients to make one, all is not lost. Use water. Although we don't recommend making delicate clear soups with water, many soups and stews, especially thick ones with plenty of flavorful vegetables or beans, can be made without stock.

Shiitake Stock

Yield: 6 cups

4–5 dried shiitake
  mushrooms

6 cups water

This simple and versatile stock works well as the basis of almost any type of soup, stew, or sauce. Besides its great taste, shiitake offers powerful healing benefits.

1. Place the shiitake in a medium-sized bowl and cover with the water. Use a small plate to keep the mushrooms submerged, and soak for at least 2 to 3 hours.

2. Remove and discard the stems from the soaked shiitake, thinly slice the caps, and return to the stock.

3. Transfer the stock to a 3-quart pot and bring to a boil. Reduce the heat to medium-low and gently simmer 15 minutes.

4. Use the stock immediately, refrigerate in a covered container for up to 5 days, or freeze for up to 6 months.

VARIATIONS

• Soak the shiitake for 15 to 20 minutes in a 3-quart pot before bringing to a boil. Reduce the heat and gently simmer for 15 minutes. If time allows, let the shiitake steep in the liquid for 30 minutes or so. Remove the shiitake and reserve for another use.

• When time is a factor, simply add the dried shiitake to the water when making the soup. When the soup is done, remove the shiitake and reserve for another use.

Kombu–Shiitake Stock

Kombu and shiitake combine to make an especially good stock. They both offer rich flavor as well as potent health benefits. As an added bonus, preparation time is short.

1. Place the shiitake, kombu, and water in a 3-quart pot and let sit for 15 minutes.

2. Place the pot over medium heat and bring to a boil. Remove the kombu, reduce the heat to medium-low, and gently simmer 10 to 15 minutes more. Remove the shiitake and reserve for another use.

3. Use the stock immediately, refrigerate in a covered container for up to 5 days, or freeze for up to 6 months.

Yield: 6 cups

4–5 dried shiitake mushrooms

6-inch piece kombu

6 cups water

Kombu–Bonito Stock

The combination of kombu and bonito results in this mild fish-flavored stock that is especially appropriate as a base for fish soups, hearty vegetable soups, and Japanese noodle broths.

1. Place the kombu and water in a 3-quart pot over medium heat and bring to a boil. Reduce the heat to medium-low and gently simmer, uncovered, for 2 to 3 minutes. Remove the kombu and reserve for another use.

2. Remove the pot from the heat, add the bonito flakes, and let sit 1 to 2 minutes. Strain the flakes from the soup, pressing any liquid back into the pot. Discard the flakes.

3. Use the stock immediately, refrigerate in a covered container for up to 5 days, or freeze for up to 6 months.

Yield: 6 cups

6-inch piece kombu

6 cups water

$1/4$ cup bonito flakes

Shellfish Stock

Yield: 4 cups

2 cups shrimp shells

1 garlic clove

2 sprigs parsley

4 cups water

Shrimp shells are perfect for making this simple delicately flavored fish stock. Any time you cook shrimp, save the shells in a freezer bag or covered container and store in the freezer.

1. Place all of the ingredients in a 3-quart pot and bring to a boil over medium heat. Reduce the heat to medium-low, cover, and simmer for 20 minutes. Strain.

2. Use the stock immediately, refrigerate in a covered container for up to 5 days, or freeze for up to 6 months.

VARIATION

For a more full-bodied stock, add any one (or more) of the following ingredients: unpeeled onion wedges, chopped celery, lemon slices or lemon juice, slices of fresh ginger root, and sprigs of fresh dill.

Vegetable Stock

Leftover vegetable trimmings and peelings, such as onion skins, wilted greens, tops of leeks and scallions, carrot and celery ends, mushroom stems, and wakame "ribs," can all be used to produce a good vegetable stock. Avoid using members of the cabbage family, such as broccoli and cauliflower, and don't use peelings that have been waxed or scraps that are spoiled. Trimmings from organic vegetables are recommended. Store the peelings and other trimmings in a container or plastic bag, and refrigerate until you have about a quart (4 cups). Keep in mind that most trimmings are highly perishable and should be used within a few days.

Yield: About 8 cups

4 cups vegetable trimmings

8 cups water

$1/2$ teaspoon sea salt

Bay leaf (optional)

2 springs fresh parsley (optional)

Flavorful herb, such as rosemary, thyme, chervil, or tarragon (optional)

1. Place all of the ingredients in a 4-quart pot and bring to a boil over medium heat. Reduce the heat to medium-low and simmer, covered, about 20 minutes. Strain the stock into another pot or large bowl.

2. Use the stock immediately, refrigerate in a covered container for up to 5 days, or freeze for up to 6 months.

VARIATION

When there are no trimmings on hand, you can still make a good stock using whole vegetables. For a basic recipe that yields 6 cups, use 1 onion that has been cut into wedges, 1 or 2 chopped carrots, 1 chopped celery rib, a few sprigs of parsley, and a bay leaf. Don't peel the vegetables. Just scrub them well and cut off the root and stem ends. Place the ingredients in a 4-quart pot with 6 cups of water, and follow the directions above.

BASIC MISO SOUPS

Instant Miso Soup

Yield: 2 to 3 servings

3 cups Shiitake Stock (page 76) or water

$1/2$ cup frozen corn

4 ounces fresh tofu, cut into $1/2$-inch cubes

$3/4$ cup coarsely chopped spinach or watercress

1 scallion, slivered

2 tablespoons red, brown rice, or barley miso

Instant miso soup mixes, which are made with miso powder, may be popular and convenient, but you can make a "fresh" instant miso soup with much more flavor in almost the same amount of time. Starting with a stock offers the best results, but water can be used as well.

1. In a 2-quart pot, bring the stock, corn, and tofu to boil over medium-high heat. Add the spinach and scallion, and simmer about 1 minute.

2. While the greens are simmering, dissolve the miso in a little of the broth. As soon as they are tender, remove the pot from the heat and stir in the miso. Serve hot.

Kyoto-Style Miso Soup

Yield: 4 servings

4 cups Kombu-Bonito Stock (page 77)

6 ounces fresh tofu, cut into $1/2$-inch cubes

2 scallions, thinly sliced

$1/4$ cup mellow white miso

Simplicity and a flavorful stock are the keys to this authentic miso soup. Traditionally served in a small bowl, this savory soup's beautiful color comes from fresh mellow white miso. Although one mellow miso can usually be substituted for another, this recipe is an exception to the rule.

1. Place the stock in a 3-quart pot and bring to a boil over medium heat. Add the tofu and scallion, reduce the heat to medium-low, and gently simmer 2 minutes. Remove from the heat.

2. Dissolve the miso in some of the broth and add it to the soup. Allow to steep a minute before serving.

Fall
Miso Soup

Fu (baked wheat gluten) adds protein and an interesting texture to this simple soup. Shonai fu, which is the variety sold in flat sheets, is recommended.

1. Place the stock and shiitake in a 4-quart pot over medium heat and bring to a boil. Reduce the heat to medium-low and simmer 5 minutes.

2. Add the squash and simmer 5 minutes.

3. Add the kale and fu and simmer 10 minutes more, or until the greens are tender. Remove from the heat.

4. Dissolve the miso in some of the broth and add it to the soup. Allow to steep a minute before serving.

Yield: 4 to 5 servings

6 cups Shiitake Stock (page 76)

4 fresh or reconstituted shiitake caps, thinly sliced

1 cup butternut squash, cut into $1/2$-inch cubes

$1^1/2$ cups tightly packed chopped kale

1 sheet shonai fu, broken into bite-sized pieces

$1/4$ cup barley, red, or brown rice miso

Summer Miso Soup

Yield: 4 to 5 servings

3–4 ears fresh corn

6 cups water

6-inch strip kombu

1 onion, diced

$1/8$ teaspoon sea salt

1 carrot, thinly sliced

2–3 tablespoons minced parsley

2 tablespoons barley, red, or brown rice miso mixed with 3 tablespoons sweet or mellow miso

Miso soup with fresh corn is our summer favorite. Boiling the cobs results in a delicious stock. When using a different summer vegetable, such as bok choy or zucchini, start with a tasty shiitake or vegetable stock.

1. Cut the corn kernels from the cobs and set them aside. Place the cobs, water, and kombu in a 4-quart pot and bring to a boil over medium heat. Reduce the heat to medium-low and gently simmer, uncovered, for 5 minutes. Remove the kombu and reserve for another use. Continue simmering the cobs 5 minutes more, then remove and discard.

2. Add the onion and salt, simmer for 10 minutes, then add the carrot and corn kernels. Continue to simmer another 10 minutes. Stir in the parsley during the last minute of cooking. Remove from the heat.

3. Dissolve the miso in some of the broth and add it to the soup. Allow to steep a minute before serving.

Winter Miso Soup

Before modern transportation enabled us to eat produce from all over the world year-round, winter soups usually featured easy-to-store root vegetables. In this typical Japanese winter soup, wakame replaces fresh greens.

1. Place the stock, daikon, and carrot in a 4-quart pot and bring to a boil over medium heat. Reduce the heat to medium-low and simmer 10 to 15 minutes, or until tender.

2. As the ingredients simmer, soak the wakame in cold or tepid water for 10 to 15 minutes. Cut away any tough ribs, and slice the fronds into 1-inch pieces.

3. Add the wakame to the pot, simmer 1 to 2 minutes, then remove from the heat.

4. Dissolve the miso in some of the broth and add it to the soup. Allow to steep a minute before serving.

Yield: 4 servings

6 cups stock*

$^{1}/_{2}$ cup julienned daikon radish

$^{1}/_{2}$ cup julienned carrot

6-inch piece wakame

$^{1}/_{4}$ cup red, brown rice, or barley miso

*Shiitake, Kombu-Shiitake, or Kombu-Bonito Stock is recommended.

Spring Miso Soup

Yield: 4 servings

4 cups stock*

6 ounces fresh tofu, cut into $\frac{1}{2}$-inch cubes

2 cups chopped watercress (1$\frac{1}{2}$-inch lengths)

3 tablespoons red, brown rice, or barley miso, or $\frac{1}{4}$ cup sweet or mellow white miso

Slivered scallions for garnish

*Shiitake, Kombu-Shiitake, or Vegetable Stock is recommended.

This soup is quick to make because the ingredients require very little cooking. Instead of watercress, you can use spinach or another light spring green.

1. Place the stock in a 4-quart pot and bring to a boil over medium heat. Reduce the heat to medium-low, add the tofu and watercress, and simmer 1 minute. Remove from the heat.

2. Dissolve the miso in some of the broth and add it to the soup. Allow to steep a minute. Garnish with scallions before serving.

A Little "Miso a Day" May Keep the Doctor Away

As detailed in Chapter 2, miso offers a significant number of health benefits, and miso soup is often taken to help restore health and/or prevent disease. When making miso soup for medicinal purposes, we always add vegetables and other foods that have well-documented healing properties. Synergistically, the following ingredients, when combined with miso in soup, as in the Ultimate Miso Soup recipe at right, pack a powerful medicinal punch.

☐ **Kombu.** A rich source of essential minerals and other nutrients, kombu is a good source of lignans and folic acid, both of which have cancer preventive properties. Kombu is also known to promote healthy thyroid function, reduce high blood pressure, and prevent heart disease.

☐ **Shiitake.** In addition to its anti-viral properties, the shiitake mushroom is also known for strengthening the immune system, reducing the risk of some cancers, and lowering cholesterol and high blood pressure.

Ultimate Miso Soup

The ingredients in this soup work together to enhance miso's medicinal benefits.

1. Combine the stock, onion, and shiitake in a 3-quart pot and bring to a boil. Reduce the heat to low and simmer 5 minutes.

2. Add the carrots and kale and simmer 8 to 10 minutes more, or until the kale is tender.

3. Add the tofu and cook for 1 to 2 minutes.

4. Dissolve the miso in some of the broth and add to the soup. Remove from the heat and steep a minute before serving.

Yield: 4 to 5 servings

6 cups Kombu-Shiitake Stock (page 77)

1 medium onion, thinly sliced in half moons

4 shiitake caps, thinly sliced

2 medium carrots, thinly sliced on the diagonal

$1^1/_2$ cups chopped kale

8 ounces fresh tofu, cut into $^1/_2$-inch cubes

4 tablespoons Hatcho miso*

*Although Hatcho (soybean) miso is recommended because it is highest in soy isoflavones, you can substitute any dark miso that lists soybeans as the first ingredient.

☐ **Onions.** The regular consumption of onions is associated with a significantly reduced risk of developing colon cancer. Onions also help lower cholesterol levels and blood pressure, reducing the risk of heart attack and stroke. They have anti-inflammatory and anti-bacterial properties as well.

☐ **Carrots.** The richest vegetable source of powerful antioxidant compounds known as *carotenoids*, carrots protect against cardiovascular disease and cancer, promote good vision, help regulate blood sugar, and enhance the immune system.

☐ **Kale.** Rich in phytonutrients that lower the risk of a variety of cancers including breast and ovarian, kale lends support to the immune system. It also helps combat anemia and prevent cataracts, heart disease, and stroke.

☐ **Tofu.** Rich in soy protein, tofu, when eaten regularly, can lower cholesterol as much as 30 percent, lower LDL ("bad" cholesterol) levels up to 40 percent, lower triglyceride levels, and reduce the formation of blood clots—greatly reducing the risk of heart disease and stroke. Tofu also alleviates the symptoms commonly associated with menopause and may inhibit post-menopausal osteoporosis.

"CREAMY" SOUPS

Cream of Corn Soup

Yield: 4 servings

2 medium leeks

2 teaspoons canola or sesame oil

3 cloves garlic, minced

1/4 teaspoon sea salt

5 cups water

3 cups frozen or cooked fresh corn kernels

1/8 teaspoon black pepper

3 tablespoons corn miso, or other sweet or mellow miso

Minced fresh cilantro for garnish

Our version of this American favorite gets its rich corn taste from both corn and corn miso; however, other varieties of mellow miso can also be used with excellent results. This recipe works well with both fresh and frozen sweet corn, although corn that has been cut fresh from the cob gives the soup a distinctly delicious flavor. When using fresh corn, be sure to use the cooking water as the stock.

1. Cut off and discard the root and the dark green fibrous portion of the leeks. Slice each leek lengthwise, cutting through only to the center (not all the way through). Wash carefully to remove any soil that may be trapped between the leaves. Cut the leeks into 1/4-inch slices and set aside.

2. Heat the oil in a 4-quart pot over low heat. Add the garlic and sauté for 1 minute or until just beginning to soften. Do not brown.

3. Add the leeks and salt, stirring briefly to coat with oil. Increase the heat to medium, add the water, and bring to a boil. Reduce the heat to medium-low, cover, and simmer for 15 minutes, or until the leeks are tender. Stir in the corn and pepper, and continue to simmer for 2 minutes.

4. Carefully ladle some of the soup into a blender until it is half full. Add the miso and blend until puréed. (Blending hot soup can be dangerous. Don't fill the blender more than half full.) Pour the purée into a large bowl, and continue to blend the remaining soup.

5. Return the puréed soup to the pot, and simmer over medium-low heat until heated through. Garnish with cilantro before serving.

Potato Leek Chowder with Roasted Garlic

The roasted garlic in this hardy classic adds a gourmet flavor that makes it a perfect choice to serve guests. The crouton and chive garnish adds just the right touch.

1. With a serrated knife, cut off and discard the root end of each head of garlic, wrap the heads in foil, and bake in a 300°F oven for 45 minutes. Remove from the oven, unwrap, and allow to cool for about 15 minutes. Squeeze the roasted garlic from the individual cloves and set aside.

2. While the garlic is roasting, cut off and discard the root and the dark green fibrous portion of the leeks. Slice each leek lengthwise, cutting through only to the center (not all the way through). Wash carefully to remove any soil that may be trapped between the leaves. Cut the leeks into ¼-inch slices and set aside.

3. Heat the oil in a 4-quart pot over medium heat. Add the leeks, potatoes, and salt, and sauté for about 2 minutes, or until the leeks begin to soften. Add the water, increase the heat, and bring to a boil. Reduce the heat to medium-low and stir in the pepper. Cover and simmer for 20 minutes, or until the vegetables are tender.

4. Carefully ladle some of the soup into a blender until it is half full. Add the thyme, roasted garlic, and miso and blend until puréed. (Blending hot soup can be dangerous. Don't fill the blender more than half full.) Pour the purée into a large bowl, and continue to blend the remaining soup.

5. Return the puréed soup to the pot, and simmer over medium-low heat until heated through. Garnish with chives and croutons before serving.

Yield: 4 servings

2 heads of garlic

3 medium leeks

1 tablespoon extra-virgin olive oil

4 medium potatoes, diced

½ teaspoon sea salt

5½ cups water

⅛ teaspoon black pepper, or to taste

1 tablespoon finely chopped fresh thyme, or ½ teaspoon dried (optional)

¼ cup sweet or mellow white miso

Chopped chives for garnish

Croutons for garnish

Creamy Carrot & Fennel Soup with Fresh Dill

Yield: 4 servings

2 medium fennel bulbs

1 tablespoon canola or
  sesame oil

1 medium onion, diced

$1/2$ teaspoon sea salt

2 medium carrots, thinly
  sliced

5 cups water

$1/8$ teaspoon black pepper,
  or to taste

2 tablespoons chopped
  fresh dill

3 tablespoons sweet or
  mellow miso

Chopped fennel or dill
  leaves for garnish

This soup's fresh taste is appealing in warm months as well as cool. Decorate it with chopped dill or fennel leaves for an attractive presentation. Be sure to use fennel with clean, white bulbs and fresh green fronds.

1. Pull off a few handfuls of the fennels' green, feathery fronds, coarsely chop, and set aside. Cut off and discard the stalks, leaving only the bulbs. Lying each bulb on its side, trim a thin slice off the root end and discard. Continue to thinly slice the bulbs and set aside.

2. Heat the oil in a 4-quart pot over medium heat. Add the onion and salt, and sauté for about 3 minutes, or until the onions are soft and translucent. Add the carrots and fennel, and sauté 2 minutes more.

3. Stir in the water, increase the heat, and bring to a boil. Reduce the heat to medium-low and stir in the pepper. Cover and simmer for 20 minutes, or until the vegetables are tender.

4. Carefully ladle some of the soup into a blender until it is half full. Add about 2 tablespoons of the chopped fennel leaves, dill, and miso, and blend until puréed. (Blending hot soup can be dangerous. Don't fill the blender more than half full.) Pour the purée into a large bowl, and continue to blend the remaining soup.

5. Return the puréed soup to the pot, and simmer over medium-low heat until heated through. Garnish with chopped fennel leaves before serving.

Creamy Squash Soup with Coconut Milk

An eclectic blend of exotic ingredients gives this soup a delightfully rich sweetness.

1. Cut off and discard the root and the dark green fibrous portion of the leeks. Slice each leek lengthwise, cutting through only to the center (not all the way through). Wash carefully to remove any soil that may be trapped between the leaves. Cut the leeks into $1/4$-inch slices and set aside.

2. Heat the oil in a 4-quart pot over medium heat. Add the leeks, squash, and salt, stirring briefly to coat with oil, and sauté for 1 minute. Add the water and coconut milk and bring to a boil. Reduce the heat to medium-low and stir in the pepper and cinnamon. Cover and simmer about 15 minutes, or until the squash is tender. Remove the cinnamon stick.

3. Carefully ladle some of the soup into a blender until it is half full. Add the ginger juice and miso, and blend until puréed. (Blending hot soup can be dangerous. Don't fill the blender more than half full.) Pour the purée into a large bowl, and continue to blend the remaining soup.

4. Return the puréed soup to the pot, and simmer over medium-low heat until heated through. Garnish with parsley before serving.

Yield: 3 to 4 servings

2 medium leeks

2 teaspoons canola or sesame oil

3 cups cubed butternut or acorn squash

$1/4$ teaspoon sea salt

$2^1/2$ cups water

14-ounce can coconut milk

$1/8$ teaspoon black pepper, or to taste

1 cinnamon stick

1 tablespoon ginger juice

3 tablespoons sweet white miso

Minced parsley for garnish

Cream of Scallion Soup

Yield: 4 servings

3 cups scallions, cut into 1-inch pieces

5 cups Shiitake Stock (see page 76)

$\frac{1}{4}$ teaspoon salt

$\frac{1}{8}$ teaspoon pepper, or to taste

3 tablespoons sweet or mellow miso

Croutons for garnish

Scallions, also called green onions, are one of the first vegetables of the spring harvest. In fact, in many cultures, scallions are considered a spring tonic after the excesses of a long winter. This version of scallion soup is quick and delicious—a great start for a spring meal.

1. Bring the stock to a boil in a 4-quart pot. Add the scallions and return to a boil. Reduce the heat to medium, cover, and simmer for 10 minutes, or until the scallions are very soft. Stir in the salt and pepper.

2. Carefully ladle some of the soup into a blender until it is half full. Add the miso and blend until puréed. (Blending hot soup can be dangerous. Don't fill the blender more than half full.) Pour the purée into a large bowl, and continue to blend the remaining soup.

3. Return the puréed soup to the pot, and simmer over medium-low heat until heated through. Garnish with croutons before serving.

Cream of Vegetable Soup with Roasted Garlic

This hearty soup is loaded with nutrition. Sweet onions, such as Vidalia or red Bermuda, are the varieties of choice. Keep in mind that the lemon juice will turn the broccoli brown, so add it just before serving.

Yield: 4 servings

2 heads of garlic

1 large stalk broccoli

1 tablespoon extra-virgin olive oil

2 medium onions, diced

3 medium carrots, diced

$1/2$ teaspoon sea salt

$5^1/2$ cups water

$1/8$ teaspoon pepper, or to taste

$1/4$ cup sweet or mellow white miso

2 tablespoons sesame tahini

1 tablespoon fresh lemon juice

Minced parsley for garnish

Croutons for garnish

1. With a serrated knife, cut off and discard the root end of each head of garlic, wrap the heads in foil, and bake in a 300°F oven for 45 minutes. Remove from the oven, unwrap, and allow to cool for about 15 minutes. Squeeze out the individual roasted garlic cloves and set aside.

2. While the garlic is roasting, cut the broccoli head from the stalk. Peel the stalk and cut into $1/2$-inch slices. Cut the head into bite-size pieces. Set aside.

3. Heat the oil in a 4-quart pot over medium heat. Add the broccoli, onions, carrots, and salt, and sauté for 2 to 3 minutes, or until the vegetables begin to soften. Add the water, increase the heat, and bring to a boil. Reduce the heat to medium-low and stir in the pepper. Cover and simmer for 20 minutes, or until the vegetables are tender.

4. Carefully ladle some of the soup into a blender until it is half full. Add the miso and tahini, and blend until puréed. (Blending hot soup can be dangerous. Don't fill the blender more than half full.) Pour the purée into a large bowl, and continue to blend the remaining soup.

5. Return the puréed soup to the pot, stir in the lemon juice, and simmer over medium-low heat until heated through. Garnish with parsley and croutons before serving.

Creamy Celery Soup

Yield: 4 servings

1 tablespoon canola oil

1 medium to large sweet onion, minced

6 stalks celery, diced

$^{1}/_{4}$ teaspoon salt

5 cups Shiitake Stock (page 76)

2 tablespoons sesame tahini

3 tablespoons sweet or mellow miso

2 tablespoons kuzu

$^{1}/_{8}$ teaspoon pepper, or to taste

Chopped parsley for garnish

Both cooling and refreshing, this is an appealing warm weather soup.

1. Heat the oil in a 4-quart pot over medium heat. Add the onion, celery, and salt, and sauté 2 to 3 minutes, or until the onion is soft and translucent. Add the stock, increase the heat, and bring to a boil.

2. Combine the tahini and miso with some of the stock, then add it to the pot. Reduce the heat to medium-low, cover, and gently simmer about 20 minutes, or until the vegetables are tender.

3. Dissolve the kuzu in 2 to 3 tablespoons cold water and stir into the soup. Continue stirring for about 3 minutes, or until the soup returns to a simmer and begins to thicken. Stir in the pepper, and simmer another minute. Garnish with parsley before serving.

Creamy Carrot Curry Soup

The heat of the curry combined with the cool creamy freshness of coconut milk results in a soup with an indescribably unique taste. This recipe calls for Madras curry—a specific hot blend from the Madras region of India—although any type will do.

1. Heat the oil in a 4-quart pot over medium heat. Add the onion and garlic, and sauté for 2 to 3 minutes, or until the onion is soft and translucent. Add the carrots and salt, and sauté another 2 minutes.

2. Stir in the water and coconut milk, increase the heat, and bring to a boil. Reduce the heat to medium-low, cover, and simmer for 20 minutes, or until the vegetables are tender. Add the curry and pepper and continue to simmer another 2 minutes.

3. Carefully ladle some of the soup into a blender until it is half full. Add the miso and blend until puréed. (Blending hot soup can be dangerous. Don't fill the blender more than half full.) Pour the purée into a large bowl, and continue to blend the remaining soup.

4. Return the puréed soup to the pot, stir in the grated carrot, and simmer over medium-low heat until heated through. Serve hot.

Yield: 4 servings

1 tablespoon extra-virgin olive oil

1 large onion, diced

3 cloves garlic, minced

4 medium to large carrots, sliced

$1/4$ teaspoon sea salt

$2^1/2$ cups water

14-ounce can coconut milk

2 teaspoons Madras curry, or to taste

$1/8$ teaspoon black pepper, or to taste

2 tablespoons sweet or mellow miso

2 tablespoons grated carrot

BEAN SOUPS

Navy Bean Soup

Yield: 6 to 8 servings

2 cups navy beans

3-inch piece kombu

10 cups water

1 teaspoon vegetable oil

1 large onion, diced

2 carrots, diced

1 rib celery, thinly sliced

1$\frac{1}{4}$ teaspoons sea salt

1 bay leaf

$\frac{1}{2}$ teaspoon summer savory

$\frac{1}{4}$ teaspoon dried thyme

$\frac{1}{4}$ cup mellow barley or
  mellow white miso mixed
  with $\frac{1}{4}$ cup water

Minced parsley for garnish

The light color and mild, slightly sweet flavor of mellow miso is a perfect match for the navy beans in this recipe.

1. Soak the beans in enough water to cover for 3 hours or overnight. Discard the soaking water and transfer the beans to a pressure cooker along with the kombu and water. Boil uncovered for 10 minutes, and skim off any foam that rises to the surface. Cover and bring to pressure, then lower the heat and cook for 1 hour, or until the beans are tender.*

2. Heat the oil in a large skillet over medium heat. Add the onion and sauté 2 to 3 minutes, or until soft and translucent. Add the carrots and celery, and sauté another 2 minutes. Reduce the heat to low, cover, and continue to cook for 10 minutes. If necessary, add a little water to prevent scorching. Remove from the heat and uncover.

3. Add the salt, bay leaf, savory, thyme, and sautéed vegetables to the cooked beans, and simmer for 20 minutes. Remove from the heat.

4. Stir the miso into the soup, cover, and let sit a minute. Remove and discard the bay leaf. Garnish with parsley before serving.

You can also prepare the soaked beans in a 6-quart pot. Increase the water to 12 cups, and the cooking time to 2 hours, or until the beans are tender. Add more water as necessary.

Pasta e Fagioli

Yield: 4 servings

Miso replaces the Parmesan cheese in this "tomato-less" variation of the traditional Italian classic. Hearty and nutritious, this pasta and bean stew needs only a side salad and whole grain bread to complete the meal.

1 cup pinto or navy beans

4-inch piece kombu

$4\frac{1}{2}$ cups water

2 teaspoons extra-virgin olive oil

1–2 cloves garlic, minced

1 onion, thinly sliced

1 large carrot, chopped

1 rib celery, thinly sliced

$\frac{1}{2}$ cup uncooked elbow macaroni

$\frac{1}{2}$ teaspoon sea salt

1 bay leaf

$\frac{1}{2}$ teaspoon oregano

Pinch black pepper (optional)

2 tablespoons red, brown rice, or barley miso mixed with 2 tablespoons water

1. Soak the beans in enough water to cover for 3 hours or overnight. Discard the soaking water and transfer the beans to a pressure cooker along with the kombu and water. Boil uncovered for 10 minutes, and skim off any foam that rises to the surface. Cover and bring to pressure, then lower the heat and cook for 1 hour, or until the beans are tender.*

2. Heat the oil in a large skillet over medium heat. Add the garlic and onion and sauté 2 to 3 minutes, or until the onion is soft and translucent. Add the carrot and celery, and sauté another 2 minutes. Reduce the heat to low, cover, and continue to cook for 10 minutes. If necessary, add a little water to prevent scorching. Remove from the heat and uncover.

3. Parboil the pasta in lightly salted water for about 5 minutes, or until it just begins to soften (do not cook completely). Drain immediately and rinse under cold running water until cool. Drain again and set aside.

4. Add the salt, bay leaf, oregano, pepper, and sautéed vegetables to the cooked beans. Simmer for 15 minutes, add the pasta, and simmer 5 minutes more. Remove from the heat.

5. Stir the miso into the pot, cover, and let sit a minute. Remove and discard the bay leaf. Serve hot.

You can also prepare the soaked beans in a 6-quart pot. Increase the water to 6 cups, and the cooking time to 2 hours, or until the beans are tender. Add more water as necessary.

Split Pea Soup

Yield: 6 servings

2 cups green split peas

8 cups water

3-inch piece kombu
  (optional)

2 teaspoons vegetable oil

1 large onion, thinly sliced
  into half moons

1 large carrot, diced

1 rib celery, thinly sliced

$1\frac{1}{2}$ teaspoons sea salt,
  or to taste

1 bay leaf

2 tablespoons red, brown
  rice, or barley miso mixed
  with 2 tablespoons water

2 tablespoons minced fresh
  basil or $\frac{1}{2}$ teaspoon dried

$\frac{1}{4}$ teaspoon ground celery
  seed (optional)

Minced parsley for garnish

Split pea soup has long been one of our family favorites, especially in the cooler months. Miso and basil gives our vegan version its rich, satisfying flavor.

1. Rinse the peas and place in a 6-quart pot along with the water and kombu, if using. Bring to a boil and skim any foam that rises to the surface. Reduce the heat to medium-low and simmer with the lid ajar for 1 to $1\frac{1}{4}$ hours, or until the peas are tender. Stir occasionally, adding more water as necessary.

2. While the peas cook, heat the oil in a large skillet over medium heat. Add the onion and sauté for 2 to 3 minutes, or until soft and translucent. Add the carrot, celery, and a small pinch of the salt, and continue to sauté another 2 minutes. Reduce the heat to low, cover, and continue to cook for 10 minutes. If necessary, add a little water to prevent scorching. Remove from the heat and uncover.

3. When the peas are tender, add the sautéed vegetables, remaining salt, and bay leaf. Stirring frequently to prevent scorching and adding water if necessary, continue to simmer the soup for 20 minutes.

4. Add the miso, basil, and celery seed, if using, and simmer another 2 minutes. Remove and discard the bay leaf. Garnish with parsley before serving.

Grandma's Lentil Soup

With eight mouths to feed, John's mother often relied on variations of this convenient, economical, and nutritious Italian-style stew. Sometimes she used chick peas or navy beans instead of lentils, and varied the vegetables depending on the season and what she had on hand.

1. Rinse the lentils and place in a 4-quart pot along with the water and slivered garlic, if using. Bring to a boil and skim any foam that rises to the surface. Reduce the heat to medium-low and simmer with the lid ajar about 40 minutes, or until the lentils are just tender. Stir occasionally, adding more water as necessary.

2. While the lentils cook, heat the oil in a large skillet over medium heat. Add the onion and minced garlic, and sauté for 2 to 3 minutes, or until the onion is soft and translucent. Add the carrot and celery, and sauté another 2 minutes. Stir in enough water to cover the vegetables along with a pinch of the salt, and simmer, covered, for 10 minutes. Remove from the heat and uncover.

3. When the lentils are tender, add the bay leaf, vegetable mixture, and remaining salt. Increase the heat, bring to a boil, and add the pasta. (If the soup is too thick for the pasta to cook, add a little water.)

4. When pasta is just tender, add the miso, basil, oregano, and half the parsley. Cover and let sit a minute. Remove and discard the bay leaf. Garnish with the remaining parsley before serving.

Yield: 6 servings

$1\frac{1}{2}$ cups lentils

5 cups water

1 clove garlic, slivered (optional)

1 tablespoon extra-virgin olive oil

1 large onion, diced

2 cloves garlic, minced

1 large carrot, diced

1 rib celery, thinly sliced

$\frac{3}{4}$ teaspoon sea salt

1 bay leaf

1 cup elbow macaroni

2 tablespoons red, brown rice, or barley miso mixed with 2 tablespoons water

1 teaspoon minced fresh basil, or $\frac{1}{4}$ teaspoon dried

1 teaspoon minced fresh oregano or marjoram, or $\frac{1}{4}$ teaspoon dried

$\frac{1}{2}$ cup minced fresh parsley

Pinto Bean Soup with Spaetzle

Yield: 6 to 8 servings

2 cups pinto beans

8 cups water

1 tablespoon extra-virgin olive oil

1 onion, diced

2 cloves garlic, minced

3 medium carrots, thinly sliced into half-moons

1 rib celery, sliced

1$\frac{1}{2}$ teaspoons sea salt

1 large bay leaf

$\frac{1}{2}$ teaspoon dried marjoram or oregano

$\frac{1}{2}$ teaspoon dried basil

2 tablespoons red, brown rice, or barley miso mixed with 2 tablespoons water

SPAETZLE

$\frac{1}{2}$ cup whole wheat flour

$\frac{1}{2}$ cup unbleached white flour

$\frac{1}{2}$ teaspoon sea salt

Pinch grated nutmeg

Pinch white or black pepper

1 egg

$\frac{1}{2}$ cup plain soymilk, almond milk, or rice milk

This hearty winter soup is enhanced with the whole grain goodness of spaetzle, a simple pasta-like dumpling. Light and puffy, spaetzle requires no kneading or rolling.

1. Soak the beans in enough water to cover for 8 hours or overnight.* Discard the soaking water and transfer the beans to a 6-quart pot along with the fresh water. Bring to a boil and skim off any foam that rises to the surface. Reduce the heat to medium, and simmer 1$\frac{1}{2}$ to 2 hours, or until the beans are tender.

2. While the beans cook, prepare the spaetzle dough. Combine the flours, salt, nutmeg, and pepper in a small bowl and mix well. In another bowl, briefly beat together the egg and soymilk. Stir the milk mixture into the flour mixture and beat well to form a thick batter. Cover the bowl with a kitchen towel and let the batter stand at room temperature for an hour.

3. Heat the oil in a large skillet over medium heat. Add the onion and garlic, and sauté 2 to 3 minutes, or until the onion is soft and translucent. Add the carrots and celery, and continue to sauté another 2 minutes. Stir in enough water to cover the vegetables and simmer, covered, for 10 minutes. Remove from the heat and uncover.

5. When the beans are tender, stir in the salt, bay leaf, marjoram, basil, and vegetable mixture. Simmer 15 minutes more, than add the miso to the soup.

6. Hold a colander with large holes over the simmering soup. Pour the spaetzle batter into the colander, then press the batter through the holes with the back of a large spoon. Simmer for 5 to 10 minutes, or until spaetzle are cooked through. Remove and discard the bay leaf. Serve hot.

To reduce soaking time, boil the beans for 2 to 3 minutes, remove from the heat, and soak 1 to 2 hours.

Azuki Bean Soup

In Japan, azuki beans have long been highly regarded for their nutritional and strengthening qualities. For centuries they have been used in the Far East as a folk remedy for kidney problems. To help restore and maintain proper blood sugar balance, traditional medicine recommends eating azuki beans with cooked pumpkin or squash.

Yield: 4 servings

1 cup azuki beans

5 cups water

1 onion, diced

$1/2$ bay leaf

Pinch rosemary

1 rib celery, sliced

$1^1/_2$ cups diced carrots, or winter squash

$1/2$ teaspoon sea salt

2 tablespoons red, brown rice, or barley miso mixed with 2 tablespoons water

$1/2$ cup minced parsley

1. Rinse the beans and place in a pressure cooker along with the water, onion, bay leaf, and rosemary. Bring to pressure, then lower the heat and cook for 50 minutes, or until the beans are tender.* Reduce the pressure and add the celery, carrots, and salt. If necessary, add a little more water. Simmer for 20 minutes.

2. Stir the miso into the pot along with half the parsley, and simmer for 2 minutes more. Remove and discard the bay leaf. Garnish with the remaining parsley before serving.

You can also prepare the soaked beans in a 4-quart pot. Increase the water to 6 cups, and the cooking time to 2 hours, or until the beans are tender. Add more water as necessary.

OTHER FAMILY FAVORITES

Mochi Soup

Yield: 5 to 6 servings

6 blocks mochi (2-x-2$\frac{1}{2}$ inches each)

1 medium burdock root

1 large carrot

8 cups Kombu-Bonito Stock (page 77)

$\frac{1}{2}$ teaspoon sea salt

8–10 button mushrooms, sliced

1 tablespoon mirin

3 scallions, cut into 1-inch pieces

4 Chinese cabbage leaves, coarsely chopped

$\frac{1}{3}$ cup sweet or mellow miso

Symbolizing longevity and wealth in Japan, mochi—a whole grain, sweet rice food—is traditionally included in the first meal of the New Year, usually in Mochi Soup (O-zoni).

1. Cut the mochi into bite-sized cubes, place on a lightly oiled cookie sheet, and bake at 350°F for 10 to 12 minutes, or until slightly brown and puffy. (Check frequently to avoid overcooking.) Set aside.

2. Cut the burdock into thin, 2-inch-long strips, and immediately place in cold water to prevent discoloration. Also cut the carrot into thin, 2-inch-long strips and set aside.

3. Drain the burdock and place in a 4-quart pot along with the stock, and bring to a boil. Add the salt, reduce the heat to medium-low, and simmer 10 to 15 minutes. Add the carrot and mushrooms and continue to simmer another 10 minutes. Stir in the mirin, scallions, and cabbage, and cook 5 minutes more.

4. When the cabbage is just tender, add the mochi to the soup. Simmer for 1 minute only, then remove from heat.

5. Dissolve the miso in some of the broth and add it to the soup. Allow to steep a minute before serving.

Caribbean Fish Chowder

This is yet another soup inspired by John Belleme, Jr. It is rich and creamy, yet fresh and stimulating. Garnished with chives, this chowder is both eye-appealing and delicious.

1. Heat the oil in a 4-quart pot over low heat. Add the garlic and sauté for 1 to 2 minutes, or until just beginning to soften. Do not brown. Add the onion and salt, and sauté for 2 to 3 minutes, or until soft and translucent. Toss in the carrots, and continue to sauté 2 minutes more.

2. Stir the water and coconut milk into the pot, then increase the heat and bring to a boil. Reduce the heat to medium, cover, and simmer about 8 minutes, or until the vegetables are tender.

3. Add the fish to the pot and cook for 5 to 10 minutes, or until the fish is cooked through.

4. Dissolve the miso in some of the broth and add it to the soup. Stir in the curry and pepper, and simmer 2 minutes more. Garnish with chives before serving.

Yield: 4 servings

1 tablespoon olive oil

4 cloves garlic, minced

1 medium onion, halved and thinly sliced into half moons

$1/4$ teaspoon sea salt

3 medium carrots, cut diagonally into $1/8$-inch slices

$2^1/2$ cups water

14-ounce can coconut milk

$1/2$ pound grouper, snapper, or orange roughy, cut into 1-inch squares

2 tablespoons mellow white miso

$1^1/2$ teaspoons Madras curry, or to taste

$1/8$ teaspoon black or white pepper, or to taste

2 tablespoons chives, chopped into 1-inch pieces

French Onion Soup

Yield: 4 servings

1 tablespoon extra-virgin olive oil

4 medium to large yellow or red Bermuda onions, halved and thinly sliced into half moons

$1/2$ teaspoon sea salt

5 to 6 cups Shiitake Stock (page 76)

2 bay leaves

3 tablespoons red, brown rice, or barley miso, or $1/4$ cup mellow white miso

2 tablespoons chopped fresh thyme

$1/8$ teaspoon pepper, or to taste

Garlic croutons for garnish

This European classic is a natural with miso. Shiitake broth gives it a meaty, full-bodied flavor, and lots of caramelized onions make it naturally sweet.

1. Heat the oil in a 6-quart pot over medium heat. Add the onions and salt, and sauté for 2 to 3 minutes, or until soft and translucent. Cover and continue to cook, stirring frequently, for 40 minutes or until the onions are browned and the juices have begun to caramelize on the bottom of the pan. If necessary to prevent burning, reduce the heat to medium-low while the onions cook.

2. When most of the liquid from the onions has evaporated and the bottom of the pot is covered with a brown natural-caramel glaze, add 3 cups of the stock. Using a wooden spoon, scrape the caramelized sugars from the bottom of the pot and stir until it is dissolved in the broth.

3. Add the bay leaves and 2 more cups of the stock, and cook over low heat for about 15 minutes. If the soup is too thick, add a little more stock.

4. Dissolve the miso in some of the broth and add it to the soup. Stir in the thyme and pepper, and simmer 1 minute more. Remove and discard the bay leaf. Garnish with croutons before serving.

Vegetable Barley Stew

Rice or barley stew seasoned with miso or umeboshi is the Japanese mother's cure-all. We enjoy this soothing stew during the colder months. It's also a staple when anyone in our family feels weak or out of balance. Make plenty— it tastes best a day or two later.

1. Rinse the barley and place in a 6-quart pot along with the shiitake, water, and kombu, if using. Soak for 3 hours. (Use a small plate or bowl to keep the mushrooms submerged.)

2. Remove the kombu and reserve for another use. Remove and discard the stems from the shiitake, thinly slice the caps, and return to the pot.

3. Bring the pot to a boil, add the salt and bay leaf, and then reduce the heat to medium-low. Simmer with the lid ajar for 45 minutes, or until the barley is tender. (Cook longer for a creamier texture.)

4. Stir in the oregano, onion, leek, carrots, and celery, and simmer another 10 minutes. Add the kale and simmer 15 minutes more. Remove from the heat.

5. Dilute the miso in a little water, add it to the soup, and let sit a minute. Remove and discard the bay leaf. Garnish with parsley before serving.

Yield: 6 servings

1 cup barley

6–8 dried shiitake mushrooms

12 cups water

6-inch piece kombu (optional)

2 teaspoons sea salt

1 bay leaf

$\frac{1}{2}$ teaspoon oregano

1 onion, diced

1 leek, white part only, thinly sliced

2 large carrots, halved lengthwise then thinly sliced into half moons

1 rib celery, sliced

2 cups chopped kale or other leafy green

3 tablespoons red, brown rice, or barley miso, or to taste

Minced parsley or slivered scallion for garnish

8. Savory Sauces

Viva la sauce! Whether a clear glistening glaze, a thick chunky purée, or a smooth and creamy gravy, a good sauce can "dress up," enhance the flavor of, and bring nutrition to a wide range of foods. Some sauces also add a heartiness that is sometimes lacking in meatless meals. Many sauces take only minutes to prepare, and, when properly stored, can keep for a number of days. It's no wonder sauces have played such an important role in eating enjoyment for centuries.

If you have always been too intimidated to make your own sauces because you associate them with complicated, time-intensive French concoctions, take heart! These types of sauces aren't as widely used as they once were. Many gourmet cooks even consider them passé.

Sauces have slowly evolved over time. During the early days of cooking, before the advent of refrigeration, thick and heavily spiced gravies were used to mask the offensive odor and taste of tainted animal foods. During the long, decadent reign of the French aristocracy, a number of palate-pleasing sauces were created to "dress up" entreés as well as desserts. Rich butter- and cream-laden affairs were among some of the more popular choices. Today's nouvelle and natural food cuisines favor simple light sauces to complement dishes, not overpower them. Sauces tend to be distinctive yet mild.

Different miso varieties can add flavor and nutritional value to a number of meatless and dairy-free sauces. Sweet and mellow misos add a dairy-like quality to light creamy sauces, while dark, longer-aged misos contribute hearty flavor to savory vegetarian gravies.

The simplest and quickest sauces to make are those that require little or no cooking and no thickening. White miso and tahini-based sauces, such as Lemon-Tahini Sauce (page 108), fall into this category, as well as sauces like Dairy-Free Pesto (page 108) and Pecan Sauce (page 109). All are easy to prepare, delicious, and nutritious.

Sauces made by thickening a well-seasoned stock with kuzu or arrowroot can be light and delicate, like Fat-Free Shiitake Sauce (page 115), or rich and hearty, like Sauce Bourguignon (page 110). Unlike meat-based gravies, these thick delicious sauces can be entirely fat-free.

Although old-fashioned, slow-cooked gravies may take a little more effort and time to prepare, there are times when no other type of sauce can fill the bill. Dark miso and the right choice of herbs can lend a meaty quality to a flavorful wine, vegetable, or shiitake stock. Flour is often used as a thickener. Recipes such as Herbed Mushroom Gravy (page 113) and "Comfort" Gravy (page 112) are delicious examples.

Whether you're looking for a simple sauce to add a lustrous glaze to your favorite steamed vegetables, or a rich savory gravy to top your favorite grain dishes, you'll find what you're looking for in this chapter. And don't be afraid to let your imagination run wild. By experi- menting with different herbs, seasonings, and stocks in the following recipes, you can easily create a wonderful array of new blends of your own.

Sauce Thickening Tips

Have you ever tried to make a sauce or gravy that either refused to thicken or, once thickened, mysteriously became thin again? If so, you're not alone. There is no doubt that the proper consistency for thickened sauces can be tricky to achieve.

Before ingredient interactions were scientifically understood, it was a common belief that sauces had to be stirred in only one direction from start to finish. At least one book on the subject even declared that left-handed people simply were not able to make a sauce successfully. Fortunately, we've learned much about the chemistry of cooking since then. When preparing your favorite gravies and sauces, the following tips will help you achieve and maintain the desired consistency.

☐ When using kuzu as a thickener, cook the miso in the sauce before adding the kuzu. Because of its starch-and protein-digesting enzymes, unpasteurized miso can sometimes thin a sauce. Simmering the miso for several minutes will ensure its pasteurization.

☐ For sauces in which the flour must first be cooked a bit before any liquid is added, stir the flour almost continuously over low heat for even cooking. If not evenly roasted, the flour's capacity to absorb the liquid will be diminished. (Do not cook the flour over high heat, which can result in a bitter taste.)

☐ When keeping a sauce warm prior to serving, do not cover the pan tightly. The steam will condense on the inside of the lid and drip back into the pan, thinning the sauce.

☐ To avoid scorching reheated sauce, dissolve it in a little hot water before reheating.

☐ Sauces thicken best when they are brought to a simmer (slightly below the boiling point) over medium-low heat. When heated to a rapid boil, they can become thin.

☐ The addition of an acidic ingredient, such as wine, vinegar, or lemon juice, to a sauce, can cause it to thin somewhat. When adding an acid, use slightly more thickener.

☐ A thick sauce will continue to thicken and form a gel as it starts to cool. For this reason, it should be a slightly thinner consistency in the pan than you want it to be at the table.

☐ If a sauce is too thick, stir in some stock or water, a little at a time, until the desired consistency is achieved.

☐ If any sauce is too thin, thicken it with a little kuzu or arrowroot that has been thoroughly dissolved in an equal amount of cold water. Stir the sauce briskly while adding the thickener, and continue stirring frequently over medium-low heat until thick.

Mellow Miso-Ginger Sauce

This is one of our favorite sauces for noodles— particularly udon. Sometimes we add a simple garnish of slivered scallions, or top the noodles with a colorful assortment of steamed vegetables.

1. Combine all of the ingredients in a 1-quart saucepan and mix well.

2. Place the pan over medium-low heat and slowly bring to a simmer, stirring frequently until the mixture thickens. Use immediately.

Yield: About 1 cup

1/3 cup water

1/4 cup sweet or mellow miso

3 tablespoons tahini

2 tablespoons brown rice vinegar or lemon juice

1 tablespoon mirin

2 teaspoons ginger juice

1 clove garlic, minced

Pinch dried tarragon or basil (optional)

Tropical Miso Sauce

No cooking is necessary for this cool, refreshing sauce that goes perfectly with blanched or lightly steamed vegetables. Broccoli, asparagus, green beans, and cauliflower are great choices. Either drizzle the sauce over the vegetables, or use it as a dip.

1. Combine all of ingredients in a small bowl and mix well.

2. Use immediately, or cover and refrigerate until ready to use.

Yield: About 1/2 cup

3 tablespoons sweet or mellow miso

5 tablespoons fresh squeezed orange juice (or to taste)

2 teaspoons tahini

1 tablespoon chopped chives or slivered scallion

Lemon-Tahini Sauce

Yield: About ²/₃ cup

6 tablespoons water

3 tablespoons tahini

2 tablespoons sweet or
  mellow miso

1 tablespoon lemon juice

*This simple sauce is surprisingly versatile and delicious.
Try it over steamed vegetables, noodles, or grains.*

1. Combine all of the ingredients in a 1-quart saucepan and
mix well.

2. Place the pan over medium-low heat and slowly bring to a
simmer, stirring frequently. Simmer for 1 minute or until thick.
Use immediately.

Dairy-Free Pesto

Yield: About ³/₄ cup

¹/₄ cup pine nuts or walnuts

1 cup tightly packed fresh
  basil leaves

¹/₄ cup fresh parsley

2 tablespoons plus 1 teaspoon
  sweet or mellow miso

2 cloves garlic, thinly sliced

¹/₂ cup extra-virgin olive oil

*You won't miss the cheese in this delicious, dairy-free version
of classic Mediterranean pesto. In addition to using this
sauce on pasta and vegetables, try it as a pizza topping.*

1. In a small, unoiled skillet, toast the pine nuts over medium
heat, stirring constantly for about 3 minutes, or until they begin
to brown slightly. Be careful not to burn.

2. Place the nuts, along with the basil, parsley, miso, garlic, and
half the oil in a blender or food processor. Purée the mixture
while slowly adding more oil through the top of the machine
until the desired consistency is reached. Use immediately.

Pecan Sauce

Walnut sauce has long been one that our family enjoys with noodles as well as vegetables. One day, we used pecans instead of walnuts and found they made an even better sauce. Since pecans lack the slight bitterness of walnuts, this sauce needs no sweetener. If, however, you use walnuts, be sure to add 1 or 2 teaspoons of mirin or rice syrup. This recipe makes enough sauce for about a pound of noodles.

Yield: About 1½ cups

2 teaspoons extra-virgin olive oil

1 small onion, diced

1–2 cloves garlic, minced

1 cup pecans

1 cup water or mild-flavored vegetable stock (carrot stock is a good choice)

3 tablespoons sweet or mellow miso

1 teaspoon lemon juice (optional)

1. In a small skillet, heat the oil over medium-low heat. Add the onion and garlic, and stir to coat with the oil. Reduce the heat to low and cover. Stirring occasionally, sauté for 15 to 20 minutes, or until the onions have caramelized to a golden brown color. If necessary, add 1 or 2 teaspoons of water to prevent burning.

2. While the onions cook, roast the pecans in an unoiled skillet over medium heat, stirring constantly for 5 to 10 minutes, or until crisp and fragrant.

3. Place all of the ingredients in a blender, and blend until smooth. Use immediately.

Sauce Bourguignon

Yield: About 3 cups

2 cups pearl onions (10 ounces), unpeeled

1¹/₂ tablespoons extra-virgin olive oil or butter

2 cloves garlic, finely minced

10–12 button mushrooms, sliced

Pinch sea salt

3 tablespoons arrowroot

1 cup dry red wine mixed with ³/₄ cup water

2 tablespoons red, brown rice, or barley miso mixed with 2 tablespoons water

¹/₂ bay leaf

¹/₄ teaspoon dried thyme

Pinch white or black pepper

Minced parsley for garnish

This robust savory sauce goes especially well over light pasta, such as artichoke ribbons or fettuccine. As it has universal appeal, Sauce Bourguignon is a perfect choice to serve guests who are not familiar with natural foods.

1. Bring 4 cups of water to boil in a 3-quart saucepan. Drop in the onions, reduce the heat to medium-low, and simmer for 10 minutes. Drain the water from the pan.

2. Cover the onions with cold water, and let sit a few minutes or until cool enough to handle. Slice the tips off the root ends, and pinch to squeeze out the onions. Set aside.

3. In a large skillet, heat the oil over medium heat. Add the garlic, mushrooms, and salt, and sauté for 5 minutes or until the mushrooms are soft. Sprinkle with arrowroot, and toss to evenly coat. While stirring briefly, add the wine.

4. Add the cooked onions to the mixture, along with the miso, bay leaf, thyme, and pepper. Continue to stir frequently for 10 minutes, or until the sauce begins to thicken somewhat.

5. Reduce heat to medium-low and simmer, loosely covered, for 15 to 20 minutes, or until the sauce is smooth and thick. Stir occasionally.

6. Remove and discard the bay leaf, and sprinkle the sauce with parsley before using.

VARIATION

For Seitan Bourguignon, simply add 1¹/₂ cups sliced seitan to the sautéing mushrooms. Lightly brown the seitan before adding the arrowroot.

Savory Brown Sauce

Flavorful stock gives this sauce its rich full-bodied taste. Enjoy it on pan-fried polenta or seitan, as well as rice, millet, or mashed potatoes.

1. To prepare the stock, place the dried shiitake in a 2-quart saucepan, add the water, and let soak for at least 20 minutes.

2. Press the cloves into the onion and add it to the pot. Simmer gently, uncovered, for 15 to 20 minutes, or until the liquid is reduced to $1\frac{1}{4}$ cups. Turn off the heat and remove the shiitake and onion, reserving them for another use.

3. In a medium-sized skillet, heat the oil over medium-low heat. Add the shallots, fresh mushrooms, and pinch of salt and pepper. Sauté about 5 minutes or until the mushrooms are soft.

4. Add the stock to the skillet, along with the wine, salt, and miso. Gently simmer, uncovered, for 10 to 15 minutes.

5. Thoroughly dissolve the kuzu in 1 tablespoon cold water, and add it to the pan while stirring briskly. Continue stirring for a minute, or until the sauce returns to a simmer and thickens. Gently simmer 1 minute more. Serve hot.

Yield: About $1\frac{1}{2}$ cups

$2\frac{1}{4}$ cups water

1–2 dried shiitake

2–3 whole cloves

1 small onion

2 tablespoons extra-virgin olive oil or butter, or combination of the two

2 shallots, minced

5–6 button mushrooms, or 3 fresh shiitake, sliced

Pinch sea salt

Pinch black pepper

1 tablespoon dry white wine or mirin

$\frac{1}{4}$ teaspoon sea salt

2 teaspoons red, brown rice, or barley miso mixed with 2 teaspoons water

1 scant tablespoon crushed kuzu

"Comfort" Gravy

Yield: About 2 cups

1 1/2 tablespoons extra-virgin olive oil

1 small onion, diced

1–2 cloves garlic, minced

3 tablespoons unbleached white flour

3 tablespoons nutritional yeast

1 1/2 cups water

3 tablespoons sweet or mellow miso mixed with 3 tablespoons water

2 teaspoons minced fresh basil, or 1/4 teaspoon dried

2 tablespoons chopped parsley

1 tablespoon white wine or mirin

This hearty gravy does as much for potatoes as Grandmother's does. It is also delicious over grains, especially bulghur and millet. The nutritional yeast adds a concentrated source of B vitamins to soothe your body and soul.

1. In a medium-sized skillet, heat the oil over medium heat. Add the onion and garlic, and sauté for 2 to 3 minutes, or until the onion is soft and translucent.

2. Reduce the heat to low. Add the flour and nutritional yeast, stirring constantly for 1 to 2 minutes.

3. Slowly add the water while stirring briskly. Increase the heat to medium, and continue to stir frequently for about 10 minutes, or until the gravy begins to simmer and thicken.

4. Reduce heat to medium-low and add the miso, basil, parsley, and wine. Stirring occasionally, simmer gently, uncovered, for 15 minutes, or until the gravy is thick and smooth. If gravy is too thick, add a little more water; if too thin, cook it down to the desired consistency. Use immediately.

Herbed Mushroom Gravy

We usually use crimini mushrooms in this gravy, but for an especially flavorful result, substitute more exotic varieties, such as chanterelles, fresh shiitake, or oyster mushrooms.

1. In a medium-sized skillet, heat the oil over medium heat. Add the onion and garlic, and sauté for 2 to 3 minutes, or until the onion is soft and translucent.

2. Add the mushrooms and a pinch of salt and pepper, and continue to sauté for 2 to 3 minutes or until the mushrooms are soft.

3. Reduce the heat to low, and sprinkle the flour over the vegetables, stirring constantly for 2 to 3 minutes.

4. Slowly add the stock while stirring briskly. Increase the heat to medium and continue to stir frequently for about 10 minutes, or until the gravy begins to simmer and thicken. Add the rest of the salt, the miso, thyme, and wine.

5. Stirring occasionally, gently simmer uncovered over medium-low heat for 15 minutes, or until the gravy is thick and smooth. Add the parsley during the last minute of cooking. Use immediately.

Yield: About 1$\frac{1}{2}$ cups

1$\frac{1}{2}$ tablespoons extra-virgin olive oil

1 small onion, diced

1–2 cloves garlic, minced

6 mushroom caps, sliced

Pinch sea salt

Pinch black pepper

3 tablespoons unbleached white or whole wheat pastry flour

1$\frac{2}{3}$ cups Vegetable Stock (see page 79)

$\frac{1}{4}$ teaspoon sea salt

2 teaspoons barley, brown rice, or red miso mixed with 2 teaspoons water

2 teaspoons fresh thyme, or $\frac{1}{2}$ teaspoon dried

1 tablespoon white wine or mirin

1 tablespoon chopped parsley

Creamy
Parsley Sauce

Yield: About 2 cups

1 cup rice milk or almond milk

$^3/_4$ cup coarsely chopped fresh parsley (loosely packed)

$^1/_4$ cup coarsely chopped fresh basil leaves* (optional)

2 tablespoons sweet or mellow miso

2 tablespoons tahini

About $^1/_2$ cup Vegetable Stock (see page 79)

$1^1/_2$ tablespoons extra-virgin olive oil

1–2 shallots, minced

$^1/_2$ small onion, minced

2 tablespoons arrowroot

$^1/_4$ teaspoon sea salt

Pinch white or black pepper

1 tablespoon mirin

1 tablespoon lemon juice

$^1/_8$ teaspoon dried basil

1 tablespoon chopped parsley for garnish

* If you choose to omit basil, increase the fresh parsley to 1 cup.

Fresh flavor and pastel green color make this creamy sauce especially appealing in spring and summer. We enjoy it over pasta.

1. Blend the rice milk, parsley, basil, miso, and tahini until smooth. Pour into a measuring cup, and add enough vegetable stock to equal 2 cups.

2. In a medium-sized skillet, heat the oil over medium-low heat. Add the shallots and onion, and sauté for 2 to 3 minutes, or until soft and translucent. Sprinkle with arrowroot, toss to evenly coat, and continue to sauté for 1 to 2 minutes.

3. Slowly add the reserved liquid, stirring constantly, until the sauce begins to thicken. Add the salt, pepper, and mirin, and gently simmer for 5 to 10 minutes.

4. Stir the lemon juice and dried basil, and cook 1 minute more. Garnish with chopped parsley before using.

Fat-Free Shiitake Sauce

Unlike most sauces or gravies, this simple recipe contains no oil or flour, yet it has a full, delicate flavor and pleasing texture. Serve it over grains, vegetables, or noodles.

Yield: About 1 2/3 cups

2 cups Kombu-Shiitake Stock (page 77)

1/4 teaspoon sea salt

1/2 bay leaf

2 fresh shiitake caps, thinly sliced

1–2 scallions, thinly sliced, or 1–2 shallots, minced

1 1/2 tablespoons red or barley miso mixed with 2 tablespoons water

2 teaspoons mirin

3 tablespoons crushed kuzu

1. Place the stock and salt in a 2-quart saucepan and simmer over medium heat. Add the bay leaf, shiitake, and scallions, and continue to simmer for 5 minutes. Stir in the miso and mirin, simmer 2 minutes more, and remove from the heat.

2. Dissolve the kuzu in 3 tablespoons cold water and slowly add it to the sauce while stirring briskly. Bring to a simmer over medium-low heat, stirring constantly for 1 to 2 minutes or until the sauce is thick.

3. Remove and discard the bay leaf before using.

Mediterranean Sweet Pepper & Onion Sauce

Yield: About 2½ cups

1 tablespoon extra-virgin olive oil

1 medium onion, halved and thinly sliced into half moons (about 1 cup)

1–2 cloves garlic, finely minced

2 medium red or green bell peppers, quartered and cut into ¼-inch strips

½ teaspoon sea salt

⅛ teaspoon white or black pepper

2 tablespoons whole wheat pastry flour, or 1½ tablespoons arrowroot

1½ cups Vegetable Stock (page 79)

2 tablespoons tomato purée or 3 tablespoons pasta sauce

2 teaspoons sweet or mellow white miso mixed with 2 teaspoons water

1 small bay leaf

Especially in mid-summer, when gardens are abundant with bell peppers, we enjoy this light vegetable sauce over seitan "steaks" or cutlets.

1. Heat the oil in a medium-sized skillet, and sauté the onion and garlic over medium-low heat for 2 to 3 minutes, or until the onion is translucent.

2. Add the bell peppers, salt, and pepper, and sauté for 2 to 3 minutes.

3. Add the flour and sauté 2 minutes more.

4. Slowly add the stock while stirring briskly. Continue stirring until the sauce thickens.

5. Add the puree, miso, and bay leaf, and simmer gently with the lid ajar for 20 to 25 minutes.

6. Remove and discard the bay leaf, adjust the seasonings, and serve.

VARIATION

When using this sauce over polenta or grain dishes, sauté some seitan strips or cubes along with the bell peppers.

Curry Sauce

We often enjoy this intensely flavorful sauce over grain dishes, although it is commonly used with shrimp, chicken, and fish. As curry powders vary greatly in flavor, you may have to try a few before finding one that suits you. Madras curry is our personal favorite.

1. In a medium-sized skillet, heat the oil over medium-low heat. Add the onion and garlic, and sauté for 2 to 3 minutes, or until the onion is soft and translucent.

2. Add the celery, and continue to sauté another 2 or 3 minutes, or until it begins to soften. Then add the salt, curry, and cumin, and sauté 1 minute more.

3. Stir in the stock and bay leaf, increase the heat to medium, and bring to a gentle simmer. Combine the miso and mirin, add it to the sauce, and continue to simmer uncovered for 20 minutes, or until the celery is tender.

4. Thoroughly dissolve the kuzu in 3 tablespoons cold water and add it to the sauce while stirring briskly. Continue stirring for 1 or 2 minutes, or until the sauce returns to a simmer and thickens. Gently simmer 1 minute more.

5. Remove and discard the bay leaf before using.

Yield: About 2¹/₂ cups

1 tablespoon extra-virgin olive oil or sesame oil

1 small onion, minced

2 cloves garlic, minced

1 rib celery, thinly sliced

1 teaspoon sea salt

1 tablespoon curry powder

1¹/₂ teaspoons cumin

3 cups Vegetable Stock (page 79)

1 bay leaf, broken in half

1 tablespoon sweet or mellow miso

1 tablespoon mirin

3 tablespoons crushed kuzu

Creamy Béchamel Sauce

Yield: About 1 1/2 cups

2 tablespoons extra-virgin
olive oil or sesame oil

2 shallots, minced, or 2
tablespoons minced onion

4 tablespoons unbleached
white or whole wheat
pastry flour

1 1/2 cups plain rice milk
or almond milk

1/2 cup water

1 scant tablespoon sweet
or mellow white miso

1 tablespoon mirin

1/2 teaspoon sea salt

1/8 cup whole parsley leaves

1/8 teaspoon white pepper

Pinch ground nutmeg
(optional)

2 teaspoons chopped fresh
basil or thyme, or 1/4
teaspoon dried (optional)

*Rice or almond milk provides a smooth, creamy texture and
richness to this dairy-free version of a French classic.*

1. In a 2-quart saucepan, heat the oil over medium-low heat.
Add the shallots and sauté for 2 to 3 minutes, or until soft and
translucent. Stirring constantly, add the flour and continue to
sauté for 3 minutes.

2. Combine the rice milk and water. Slowly add it to the pan
while whisking. Increase the heat to medium, stirring frequently until the mixture begins to thicken.

3. Combine the miso and mirin, and add it to the sauce along
with the salt, parsley, and pepper. Gently simmer for 20 minutes. Add nutmeg and basil, if desired, and simmer 1 to 2 minutes more.

4. Strain the sauce through a fine sieve. If too thick, add a little
more water and reheat before serving.

Ginger–Miso Marinade

Marinate shrimp or other seafood in this flavorful marinade for 45 to 60 minutes. Try it when preparing Shrimp Japonais (page 170).

1. Combine all of the ingredients in a medium-sized bowl and mix well.

2. Use immediately, or cover and refrigerate until ready to use.

Yield: About ½ cup

3 tablespoons sweet or mellow miso

3 tablespoons mirin

2 tablespoons sake or dry white wine

2 teaspoons ginger juice

1 teaspoon shoyu

Universal Marinade

The American Miso Company shared this versatile marinade with us. It's great for flavoring fish, poultry, tofu, tempeh, and vegetables before grilling, broiling, or roasting.

1. Combine all of the ingredients in a medium-sized bowl and mix well.

2. Use immediately, or cover and refrigerate until ready to use.

Yield: About 1 cup

¼ cup red, barley, or brown rice miso

6 tablespoons mirin

6 tablespoons dry red wine

2 tablespoons brown rice vinegar

2 teaspoons toasted sesame oil

2 cloves garlic, minced

1 tablespoon finely grated fresh ginger

9. Eat Your Vegetables!

From crimson red bell peppers and forest green broccoli to golden squash and snow-white daikon radishes, vegetables provide a dazzling assortment of colors that can make everyday meals feasts for the eyes. Their wide array of flavors and textures further stimulates and satisfies the senses. And let's not forget that fresh vegetables are low-calorie storehouses of essential vitamins, minerals, and fiber. Including miso in their preparation—in combination with ingredients such as lemon juice, tahini, rice vinegar, and mirin—adds additional interest, flavor, and nutritional value. Yes, there are plenty of good reasons to eat your vegetables!

In general, the light, sweet misos are preferred over dark varieties for flavoring vegetable dishes. They enhance without overpowering, allowing the colors and natural flavors of the vegetables to come through. Sweet and mellow misos have the added advantage of being significantly lower in salt than dark misos. Although most of the dishes in this chapter contain light, often creamy miso sauces, there are a few, such as Green Beans in Sesame Miso (page 127) and Curried Zucchini and Yellow Squash with Slivered Almonds (page 132), that taste best when stronger-flavored dark misos are combined with more robust seasonings.

Vegetables dishes that are flavored with miso sauces or dressings should be eaten right away. Shortly after miso is combined with cooked vegetables, its enzymatic activity alters their flavor, color, and texture. You can, however, prepare the sauce ahead of time—just don't combine it with the vegetables until you are ready to serve the dish.

When choosing vegetables, freshness is key. As soon as they are harvested, vegetables begin to lose their flavor, texture, and nutritional value. Although it is ideal to buy locally grown vegetables that are in season, in many parts of the country this is unrealistic. However, when shopping for produce, never settle for tired, wilted fruits and vegetables; they offer little energy. Choose items that are crisp and fresh, and use them within a few days. Also, whenever possible, select organic produce over nonorganic varieties. Research has shown that organic vegetables, which are grown without pesticides, offer significantly more vitamins and minerals than their conventionally grown counterparts. Nonorganic vegetables are subject to a variety of objectionable practices even after they've been harvested. To extend their shelf life, for example, many are washed in water that has been treated with fungicides, while others are irradiated. For a fresher appearance, several vegetables, including tomatoes, peppers, and summer squash, are coated with wax, which is difficult to remove. Some vegetables, tomatoes in particular, are picked before they are ripe and then gassed with a synthetic chemical to speed ripening. Although organic produce may cost a little more than nonorganic, the additional pennies are a wise investment in both your health and the health of the planet.

In addition to selecting fresh organic produce for optimal flavor and nutrition, the method and length of cooking also play a part. Although cooking most vegetables increases their nutrient absorbability, overcooking greatly diminishes their nutritional value, color, and texture. In general, vegetables should be cooked just until they are tender-crisp. Steaming, parboiling or blanching, and stir-frying are recommended methods for most vegetables, although lengthy boiling in salted water is necessary for tough vegetables like turnips and rutabaga, as well as bitter ones such as broccoli raab. When parboiling green vegetables, adding a little salt to the water helps preserve their bright, appetizing color. To maintain their color during steaming, add green vegetables to the steamer *after* the water has come to a full boil and the steam is rising. As soon as the vegetables are cooked, remove them from the pot or steamer. You can also run them under cold water, which will stop the cooking process and set their color.

You'll find all of the following recipes to be satisfying and delicious. For the most part, they take little time to prepare and feature common vegetables that are readily available.

Spinach Citrus Surprise

This attractive side dish is nutritious and simple to prepare. Be sure to thoroughly wash the fresh spinach leaves, which are grown in sandy soil and can be very gritty.

1. Combine the sauce ingredients and half the scallions in a small bowl. Set aside.

2. In a small unoiled skillet, toast the sesame seeds over medium heat, stirring constantly, for 1 to 2 minutes, or until they are fragrant and begin to pop. Remove from the heat and set aside.

3. Heat the oil in a 4-quart pot over medium heat. Add the garlic and remaining scallions, and sauté for about 1 minute, or until the scallions are beginning to wilt and the garlic begins to soften.

4. Add the spinach to the pot and cover. Stirring occasionally, cook for 2 to 3 minutes or until the spinach is wilted yet still bright green. Remove from the heat, drain any excess liquid, and transfer to a serving bowl. Add the sauce, and toss to evenly coat.

5. Sprinkle with sesame seeds and serve.

Yield: 4 servings

2 scallions, chopped

$1^1/_2$ teaspoons sesame seeds

1 teaspoon light sesame or canola oil

2 cloves garlic, minced

10 ounces fresh spinach leaves, cleaned and stemmed

CITRUS-MISO SAUCE

$1^1/_2$ tablespoons sweet or mellow white miso

2 tablespoons orange juice

$^1/_4$ teaspoon toasted sesame oil

$^1/_4$ teaspoon lemon juice

Green Beans Amandine

Yield: 4 servings

2 teaspoons sesame or
 safflower oil

$^1/_3$ cup slivered almonds

$3^1/_2$ cups green beans, thinly
 sliced on the diagonal
 (French style)

Pinch sea salt

3 tablespoons sweet or
 mellow miso

3 tablespoons mirin

Flavorful miso-mirin sauce transforms plain green beans into a dish that's anything but plain! This sauce is also great with sliced asparagus and shredded cabbage.

1. Heat the oil in a medium-sized skillet over medium heat. Add the almonds and sauté for 2 to 3 minutes, or until just beginning to turn golden brown.

2. Add the green beans and salt, and continue to sauté another 1 to 2 minutes.

3. Add enough water to just cover the bottom of the skillet, cover, and steam the beans for 10 to 15 minutes, or they are bright green and tender-crisp.

4. Combine the miso and mirin, add to the skillet, and toss with the beans. Cook another minute, adding a little more water if needed.

5. Immediately transfer to a serving bowl and enjoy.

Gingered Carrots and Sugar Snap Peas

Kuzu sauce adds an appetizing sheen to this colorful vegetable duo.

1. Heat the oil in a medium-sized skillet over medium heat. Add the carrots and salt, and toss to evenly coat with oil. Sauté for 1 minute. Add the water, cover, and cook for 5 minutes, or until the carrots begin to soften.

2. Toss the snap peas into the skillet, cover, and cook about 4 minutes, or until tender-crisp. Remove from the heat.

3. If there is any liquid in the skillet, spoon it into a measuring cup along with the mirin and enough water to equal $\frac{1}{3}$ cup. Add the miso and ginger juice, and stir to blend well.

4. Thoroughly dissolve the kuzu in 1 tablespoon cold water, and add to the miso mixture. Pour the mixture over the vegetables in the skillet, and place over medium heat.

5. Stirring constantly, heat the ingredients until the sauce thickens and becomes translucent. Reduce the heat to low and let simmer for 1 minute.

6. Transfer the vegetables to a serving bowl and enjoy hot.

Yield: 4 servings

1–2 teaspoons safflower or light sesame oil

2 large carrots, halved lengthwise and diagonally cut into $\frac{1}{8}$-inch slices

Pinch sea salt

$\frac{1}{4}$ cup water

4 ounces sugar snap peas, strings removed

2 tablespoons mirin

1 tablespoon sweet or mellow miso

$\frac{1}{2}$ teaspoon fresh ginger juice

2 teaspoons crushed kuzu

1 tablespoon cold water

Vegetables au Gratin

Yield: 4 servings

3-inch piece kombu

3 large carrots, cut into bite-sized chunks

Pinch sea salt

$1/4$ head cabbage, cut crosswise into $1/2$-inch slices

2 large parsnips, cut into bite-sized chunks

2 cups broccoli florets

$1/4$ cup sweet or mellow miso

3 tablespoons mirin

1 cup Instant Tofu "Cheese" (page 153)

1 cup breadcrumbs

Minced parsley for garnish

Making this hearty cold-weather dish may appear complicated, but it's actually quite simple. When short on time, you can omit the tofu "cheese" and breadcrumbs.

1. In a large skillet set over medium heat, add the kombu, carrots, salt, and $1/4$-inch of water. Cover and simmer for 5 minutes. Add the cabbage, and simmer another 5 minutes.

2. Add the parsnips to the skillet, and continue to simmer for 15 minutes, or until all of the vegetables are just tender.

3. While the parsnips are cooking, bring 4 cups of water to a boil in a 2-quart pot, add a pinch of salt and parboil the broccoli for 4 to 5 minutes, or until tender-crisp. Drain immediately and set aside.

4. Add the miso to the mirin, mix until well blended, and add to the skillet with the simmering vegetables. If, before adding the miso mixture, the liquid in the skillet had evaporated, *also* stir in 2 to 3 tablespoons of water. Add the broccoli, toss all of the ingredients together, and simmer another minute.

5. Transfer the vegetables to an ungreased casserole or cake pan. Top with dollops of tofu "cheese," and sprinkle with breadcrumbs. Place the casserole under a preheated broiler for 3 minutes, or until the top is lightly browned.

6. Garnish with parsley and serve.

Green Beans in Sesame-Miso

Quick and easy to prepare, this dressing adds rich flavor and nutrition to most lightly steamed or blanched vegetables.

1. Bring 4 cups of water and the salt to boil in a 3-quart pot. Add the green beans and parboil for 10 minutes, or until bright green and tender-crisp. Drain and place in a serving bowl.

2. In a small unoiled skillet, toast the sesame seeds over medium heat, stirring constantly for 1 to 2 minutes, or until they are fragrant and begin to pop. Transfer the seeds to a suribachi or mortar, and grind well. Add the oil and miso, and mix together until well blended. Stir in the mirin, lemon juice, and rice syrup to produce a thick, dry, somewhat coarse dressing.

3. Add the dressing to the green beans, toss gently to evenly coat, and serve.

Yield: 4 servings

Pinch sea salt

3 cups green beans, cut diagonally into 1$\frac{1}{2}$-inch pieces

3 tablespoons sesame seeds

1 teaspoon light sesame oil

2 tablespoons red, brown rice, or barley miso

1 tablespoon mirin

1 teaspoon lemon juice

1 tablespoon rice syrup, or $\frac{1}{2}$ tablespoon honey

Broccoli with Pecan Sauce

Attractively arranged on a platter, bright green broccoli florets surround a bowl of creamy pecan miso dipping sauce. A great choice for the buffet table.

1. Bring 6 cups of water and the salt to a boil in a 4-quart pot. Add the broccoli and parboil for 4 to 5 minutes, or until bright green and tender-crisp. Drain immediately and set aside.

2. Put the Pecan Sauce in a bowl and place in the center of a serving platter. Arrange the broccoli florets around the bowl and serve.

Yield: 4 to 5 servings

Pinch sea salt

6 cups broccoli florets

1$\frac{1}{2}$ cups Pecan Sauce (page 109)

"Scalloped" Parsnips

Yield: 3 servings

2 teaspoons vegetable oil

1 large onion, halved and
  thinly sliced into half
  moons

3–4 medium-sized parsnips

Pinch sea salt

2 tablespoons sweet or
  mellow miso

2 tablespoons mirin

Chopped chives for garnish

Although parsnips rarely make it to the top of anyone's "most popular vegetable" list, this dish is likely to elevate their status.

1. In a medium-sized skillet, heat the oil over medium heat. Add the onion and sauté for 2 to 3 minutes, or until soft and translucent. Reduce the heat to low, cover, and slow-cook the onions for 15 to 20 minutes, or until they are very tender and sweet.

2. While the onions cook, cut the parsnips diagonally into $\frac{1}{8}$-inch-thick slices. Add the parsnips and salt to the onions and toss. Add enough water to just cover the bottom of the skillet, cover, and simmer for 10 minutes, or until the parsnips are just tender.

3. In a small bowl, combine the miso and mirin, and stir to blend well. Pour the mixture over the parsnips and toss gently. Simmer another 2 to 3 minutes, or until the parsnips are completely tender.

4. Transfer to a serving bowl, garnish with chives, and enjoy!

Vegetable Medley with Lemon-Tahini Sauce

Quick and easy-to-prepare, Lemon-Tahini Sauce is a perfect complement to this colorful vegetable combo.

1. Place the carrots in a steamer basket or on a steamer rack set over boiling water. Cover and steam for 5 minutes. Add the cauliflower to the carrots, and continue to steam for 5 minutes. Add the broccoli, and steam for another 5 to 7 minutes, or until it is bright green and tender-crisp.

2. Transfer the vegetables to a serving bowl, add the sauce, and toss gently. Serve immediately.

Yield: 5 to 6 servings

3 medium carrots, cut into bite-sized wedges

3 cups cauliflower florets

3 cups broccoli florets

$^2/_3$ cup Lemon-Tahini Sauce (page 108)

Broccoli a l'Orange

Tropical Miso Sauce gives this simple side dish a fresh, snappy taste. It's also great with asparagus, green beans, and cauliflower.

1. Bring 6 cups of water and the salt to boil in a 4-quart pot. Add the broccoli and parboil for 4 to 5 minutes, or until bright green and tender-crisp. Drain immediately.

2. Place the broccoli on a platter and top with the sauce. You can also use the Tropical Miso as a dipping sauce for the florets.

Yield: 4 to 5 servings

Pinch sea salt

5 cups broccoli florets

$^1/_2$ cup Tropical Miso Sauce (page 107)

Sugar Snap Peas with Fresh Mint

Yield: 4 to 5 servings

4 cups sugar snap peas, trimmed and strings removed

1 tablespoon olive oil

2 teaspoons sweet or mellow white miso

2 teaspoons lemon juice

1½ tablespoons thinly slivered fresh mint

Sugar snaps are edible pod peas and one of the earliest vegetables to mature in spring. This dish combines their natural sweetness with the refreshing flavors of lemon and mint.

1. Place the peas in a steamer basket or on a steamer rack set over boiling water. Cover and steam for 4 to 5 minutes, or until bright green and tender-crisp. Transfer to a bowl of cold water to cool. Drain and set aside.

2. In a small bowl, combine the oil, miso, and lemon juice, and stir until well blended. Add the mint.

3. Place the peas in a serving bowl, top with the miso mixture, and toss to coat. Serve immediately.

VARIATION

For a delightful variation of this dish with a completely different flavor, substitute 1 tablespoon each of fresh basil and fresh parsley for the mint.

Cauliflower with Sesame-Ginger Vinaigrette

Tasty vinaigrette gives the cauliflower an authentic Asian flavor in this delectable dish. Be careful not to overcook the florets or they will fall apart.

1. Combine all of the vinaigrette ingredients in a small bowl and stir vigorously until well blended. Set aside.

2. Place the cauliflower in a steamer basket or on a steamer rack set over boiling water. Cover and steam for 7 to 10 minutes, or until tender-crisp. Drain well and place in a serving bowl.

3. Stir the vinaigrette, pour over the cauliflower, and toss to coat. Sprinkle with sesame seeds and serve.

Yield: 4 servings

6 cups cauliflower florets

1 tablespoon lightly toasted sesame seeds

SESAME-GINGER VINAIGRETTE

2 tablespoons sweet or mellow miso

1 tablespoon toasted sesame oil

1 tablespoon lemon juice

1$\frac{1}{2}$ teaspoons fresh ginger juice

1 small clove garlic, minced (optional)

Curried Zucchini and Yellow Squash with Slivered Almonds

Yield: 4 servings

2 small zucchini, sliced into $1/4$-inch rounds (3 cups)

2 small yellow crookneck squash, sliced into $1/4$-inch rounds (3 cups)

1 tablespoon ghee or extra-virgin olive oil

1 tablespoon garam masala

Pinch black or white pepper

$1/2$ teaspoon ground coriander

$1/2$ cup slivered almonds

2 tablespoons sweet or mellow miso

$1/4$ cup almond or rice milk

2 teaspoons mirin

This variation of an Indian vegetable curry dish has a bold, mildly spicy flavor. Garam masala, a flavorful blend of aromatic spices, and ghee, clarified butter, are available in most natural foods stores and shops that sell Indian foods.

1. Place the zucchini and yellow squash in a steamer basket or on a steamer rack set over boiling water. Cover and steam for 5 minutes, or until tender-crisp. Do not overcook. Remove from the heat and set aside.

2. In a large skillet, heat the ghee over medium-low heat. Add the garam masala, pepper, and coriander, and stir to combine with the oil. Add the almonds, and sauté for 3 to 5 minutes, or until slightly brown.

3. In a small bowl, combine the miso, almond milk, and mirin, and stir until well blended.

4. Add the squash and miso mixture to the skillet, and gently toss all of the ingredients together. Transfer to a serving bowl and enjoy hot.

10. Pasta East and West

Delicious and nutritious, pasta is a culinary favorite in both Eastern and Western cuisines. A wide variety of high quality pastas, now available to health-conscious consumers, is just what the Surgeon General ordered. Pasta's "time-released" energy from the slow metabolism of its complex carbohydrates supplies a constant stream of glucose (blood sugar) to fuel the body. One four-ounce serving of durum wheat or buckwheat (soba) pasta contains about fifteen grams of high-quality protein with only about 400 calories. What's more, whole grain rice, buckwheat, and durum pastas are a good source of fiber, amino acids, iron, and B vitamins. When accompanied by legumes and/or vegetables, and topped with certain sauces, pasta can be the backbone of a nutritious, low-calorie cuisine.

Miso, which has long been used in a variety of Asian noodle dishes, is gaining popularity in Western pasta dishes as well. Sweet and mellow misos are especially well-suited for pasta sauces and dressings. John's mother, a second-generation Italian-American, has been making pasta sauce since she was a young child. Several years ago, she began experimenting by adding miso to her spaghetti sauce, and found that sweet miso mellows the acidity and improves the flavor. She has been adding miso to her sauce ever since. If you desire a creamy white sauce that's low-fat and dairy-free, light misos can fill the bill. For more robust or highly seasoned fare, dark misos are preferred.

COOKING ITALIAN-STYLE PASTA

The Italian-style dry pastas that are popularly used in Western cuisine are made from semolina, a protein-rich flour milled from the heart of high-gluten durum wheat. They contain no salt or eggs and come in a variety of shapes and sizes. In recent years, natural foods companies began offering hearty Italian-style pastas made from whole durum wheat as well as smooth-textured semolina-artichoke varieties. A few are wheat-free and some have added vegetable powders or herbs.

Essentially, all Italian-style pastas are cooked the same way. Use plenty of water—about three to four quarts per pound of pasta. Once the water comes to a rolling boil, add about a tablespoon of salt. Without salt, even the best pasta will taste bland. Once the pasta is added to the boiling water, stir briefly to prevent the noodles from sticking together. Then cover the pot until the water returns to a rapid boil, uncover, and cook the pasta just until it is firm and chewy (*al dente*). Cooking time will vary considerably for different varieties, so test frequently to prevent overcooking. Immediately drain the cooked pasta in a colander and then transfer to a heated bowl. Top with the sauce and toss to coat. Serve immediately while still hot.

Although cooking pasta is simple, it requires attention and careful timing. Italian-style pasta should not be overcooked, overdrained, or allowed to sit for more than a minute or two before being served. Because of this, it is important to have the sauce and any other added ingredients ready when the pasta is done cooking.

COOKING JAPANESE-STYLE PASTA

In Japan, packages of udon and somen (wheat pastas) and soba (buckwheat pasta) are as common in kitchen cupboards as spaghetti and macaroni are in the West. Udon and somen are long noodles that are available in both whole wheat and sifted wheat varieties. The only difference is that somen is cut into thinner strands than udon. Soba is also a long, thin noodle. Some varieties are made from 100 percent buckwheat flour, but most contain from 20 to 60 percent wheat flour. Ingredients such as green tea powder, dried mugwort leaves, and jinenjo (wild mountain yam) are often added to the basic soba dough.

Although Japanese pastas, like Italian varieties, are made from flour and water, they are cooked and served quite differently. The wheat that is used to make udon and somen (and blended with buckwheat to make soba) is less glutinous than the durum wheat used in Italian pasta. Salt is also added to most varieties of Japanese pasta dough for improved flavor and texture, and the noodles are most commonly served in a shoyu or miso-seasoned broth. Since they are less dense and more porous than Italian pastas, udon and soba are perfectly suited to absorb the flavor of thin broths. They also go well with various miso sauces, and can be tossed with vegetables and dressings to make pasta salads.

The method of cooking Japanese pastas differs from Italian in two important ways: First, it is not necessary to add salt to the cooking water because salt is already included in the dough (salt-free 100-percent soba is an exception). Second, Japanese noodles are drained and immediately rinsed under cold running water, or submerged in a bowl of cold water until the noodles are cool enough to handle. The noodles are then drained again. Cooked Japanese noodles that have been drained and sitting too long may become a little dry. When using them in salads or other recipes that are not hot, simply rinse them under cold water and drain again before serving. If reheating is necessary in a particular recipe, undercook the noodles slightly. Then just before serving, briefly dip them into boiling water or broth, one serving at a time until just heated through.

As with Italian pasta, test Japanese noodles frequently as they cook. The noodles should be chewy, never mushy. When bitten in half, they should be uniform in color.

The recipes in this chapter range from traditional Japanese dishes such as Somen in Miso Broth (page 136) to updated, dairy-free versions of popular Western dishes, like creamy Pasta Primavera (page 145) and Italian-Style Stuffed Shells (page 146). Unless otherwise specified, servings are main-dish portions. In addition to these offerings, there are a variety of recipes in other chapters, especially the salad dressings in Chapter 6 and the sauces in Chapter 8, that you can use to create your own pasta dishes. For example, simply combine your choice of pasta with Dairy-Free Pesto (page 108) or Sauce Bourguignon (page 110). Or toss together a colorful assortment of raw or blanched vegetables with some cooked macaroni and Basil Vinaigrette (page 63) for a tasty and nutritious salad. When it comes to pasta and miso, the possibilities are limitless!

Udon in White Miso–Sesame Broth

Although this Japanese-style pasta dish calls for udon noodles, it works just as well with whole wheat somen. The rich, cream-colored broth is both delicious and nutritious.

Yield: 2 servings

1/4 sheet nori, toasted

8 ounces udon noodles

1/4 cup hulled white sesame seeds

1/4 cup sweet or mellow miso

3 cups Kombu-Bonito Stock or Kombu-Shiitake Stock (page 77)

1/4 teaspoon sea salt

1 tablespoon mirin

2 teaspoons ginger juice

Slivered scallions for garnish

1. Using a scissors, cut the nori into 1-inch-wide strips, and then cut the strips into slivers. Set aside.

2. In a 4-quart pot, bring 2 quarts of water to a rolling boil. Add the noodles and cook until al dente. Immediately drain the noodles and rinse under cold running water, or submerge in a bowl of cold water for 30 seconds or until cool. Drain and set aside.

3. Place the sesame seeds in a dry skillet set over medium-low heat. Stir constantly for about 2 minutes, or until the seeds are fragrant and just beginning to turn golden. Be careful not to burn. Immediately transfer the seeds to a suribachi or mortar and crush well. Add the miso and 1/2 cup of the stock. Mix well to thoroughly dissolve the miso.

4. Place the sesame-miso mixture in a 2-quart pot along with the salt, mirin, ginger, and the remaining stock. Bring just to a simmer and remove from the heat.

5. Divide the cooked noodles in individual serving bowls, and add enough broth to almost cover. Garnish with nori and scallions, and serve.

Somen in Miso Broth

Yield: 2 to 3 servings

8 ounces somen noodles

3 cups Kombu-Bonito Stock
(page 77)

1 carrot, cut into matchsticks

6 ounces tofu, cut into
$1/2$-inch cubes

$1/2$ cup chopped scallions

5 tablespoons mellow white
miso

Thin and light, somen noodles are perfectly suited for this traditional Japanese dish, which is typically served for lunch.

1. In a 4-quart pot, bring 2 quarts of water to a rolling boil. Add the noodles and cook until al dente. Immediately drain the noodles and rinse under cold running water, or submerge in a bowl of cold water for 30 seconds or until cool. Drain and set aside.

2. In a 2-quart pot, bring the stock to a simmer. Add the carrots, and simmer for 5 to 7 minutes. Stir in the tofu and half the scallions, and simmer another 4 to 5 minutes. Remove from the heat.

3. In a small bowl, dissolve the miso in about $1/2$ cup of the broth, then add to the pot.

4. Divide the noodles in individual serving bowls. Ladle the soup into individual soup bowls, filling them two-thirds full. Garnish with the remaining scallions.

5. Grab a few noodles with chopsticks or a fork, then dip in the broth and eat. When the noodles are gone, drink the remaining broth.

Japanese-Style Fried Noodles

Unlike Chinese-style fried noodles, this recipe uses less oil. The cooked noodles are briefly sautéed and then tossed with a simple sauce.

1. In a 4-quart pot, bring 2 quarts of water to a rolling boil. Add the noodles and cook until al dente. Immediately drain the noodles and rinse under cold running water, or submerge in a bowl of cold water for 30 seconds or until cool. Drain and set aside.

2. Combine the miso and mirin in a small bowl. Set aside.

3. Heat the oil in a large skillet over medium heat. Add the shallot and sauté for 1 minute, or until it just begins to soften. Add the noodles, increase the heat to medium-high, and sauté for 30 to 60 seconds.

4. Add the miso-mirin mixture and toss to coat the noodles evenly (if too dry, add a little water.) Sauté 1 minute more.

5. Sprinkle with scallions and serve immediately.

Yield: 2 to 3 servings

8 ounces udon noodles

3 tablespoons sweet or mellow miso

3 tablespoons mirin

1 tablespoon sesame oil or toasted sesame oil

2 tablespoons minced shallot, or 1 tablespoon minced garlic

Slivered scallion for garnish

Noodles with Pecan Sauce

Yield: 4 servings

1 pound udon, soba, or whole wheat somen noodles

1$^1/_2$ cups Pecan Sauce (page 109)

Slivered scallion for garnish

Here's a simple yet flavorful entrée that is popular with kids and adults alike. For a complete meal, top the noodles with a colorful assortment of steamed vegetables.

1. In a 6-quart pot, bring 3 to 4 quarts of water to a rolling boil. Add the noodles and cook until al dente. Immediately drain the noodles and rinse under cold running water, or submerge in a bowl of cold water for 30 seconds or until cool. Drain well.

2. Divide the noodles among four shallow bowls or plates. Spoon the sauce over the noodles, garnish with scallions, and serve.

Noodles with Mellow Miso-Ginger Sauce

Yield: 2 servings

8 ounces udon or whole wheat somen noodles

1 cup Mellow Miso-Ginger Sauce (page 107)

Minced scallion for garnish

This simple dish is one of our family favorites and a great choice when a quick-and-easy meal is called for. Serve it with a simple garnish of scallions or topped with a colorful assortment of your favorite steamed vegetables.

1. In a 4-quart pot, bring 2 quarts of water to a rolling boil. Add the noodles and cook until al dente. Immediately drain the noodles and rinse under cold running water, or submerge in a bowl of cold water for 30 seconds or until cool. Drain and set aside.

2. Divide the noodles among two serving bowls, top with the sauce, and garnish with scallions. Serve immediately.

Noodles with Marinated Tofu-Vegetable Topping

This delicious dish is a cold-weather favorite.

1. Combine the marinade ingredients in a medium-sized bowl, and set aside.

2. Soak the tofu in lukewarm water for 5 to 10 minutes to soften. Press each cake firmly between your hands to squeeze out the water. Rinse and press several times until the water runs clear. Dice the tofu and add it to the marinade, tossing to coat evenly. Marinate for 45 to 60 minutes, tossing occasionally.

3. While the tofu marinates, cut off and discard the root and the dark green fibrous portion of the leek. Slit the leek lengthwise, cutting through only to the center (not all the way through). Wash carefully to remove any soil that may be trapped between the leaves, then thinly slice on the diagonal.

4. In a 4-quart pot, bring 2 quarts of water to a rolling boil. Add the noodles and cook until al dente. Immediately drain the noodles and rinse under cold running water, or submerge in a bowl of cold water for 30 seconds or until cool. Drain and set aside.

5. Heat the oil in a wok or large skillet over medium-low heat. Add the onion and garlic, and sauté for 2 minutes, or until the onion is just translucent. Add the carrot and sauté another 2 minutes, then add the leek and sauté 2 minutes more.

6. Toss the tofu into the wok along with the marinade, mirin, and 1 cup of the stock. Cover and simmer for 10 minutes, then stir in the remaining stock.

7. Thoroughly dissolve the kuzu in 1 to 2 tablespoons of water, then add to the wok while stirring briskly. Gently simmer 1 to 2 minutes, or until the sauce has thickened.

8. Place the noodles in individual bowls, top with the tofu-vegetable mixture, and serve.

Yield: 3 servings

5 cakes dried tofu

1 leek

12 ounces udon or whole wheat somen noodles

2 tablespoons sesame oil

1 red onion, thinly sliced

2 cloves garlic, minced

1 carrot, cut into julienne strips

1 tablespoon mirin, sake, or dry white wine

1 1/2 cups Shiitake Stock (page 76), or water

1 level tablespoon crushed kuzu

MARINADE

1/4 cup mirin

2 tablespoons barley, red, or brown rice miso

2 tablespoons sweet or mellow miso

1 tablespoon brown rice vinegar

1 tablespoon ginger juice

1 teaspoon shoyu or tamari

Festive
Noodle Salad

Yield: 4 servings

5.3 ounce package bifun noodles

1 large carrot, cut into matchsticks

About 20 snow peas, strings removed

1½ cups broccoli florets

2 cups watercress, stems removed

DRESSING

⅓ cup orange juice

2 tablespoons sweet or mellow miso

2 tablespoons tahini

1 heaping tablespoon chopped scallion

1 tablespoon lemon juice

This delicious, eye-appealing noodle salad is perfect to serve on a hot summer day. Bifun, a Chinese-style rice noodle is thin, light, and the ideal choice for this dish, although somen is a good substitute.

1. In a 4-quart pot, bring 2 quarts of water to a rolling boil. Add the noodles and cook until al dente. Immediately drain the noodles and rinse under cold running water, or submerge in a bowl of cold water for 30 seconds or until cool. Drain and set aside.

2. In a pot of lightly salted water, parboil the vegetables individually. Begin with the carrots, letting them cook for about 1 minute. Remove with a slotted spoon and transfer to a colander. Rinse with cold water, drain, and set aside. Cook the snow peas for 30 seconds, the broccoli for 3 minutes, and the watercress for 15 seconds, or until just wilted.

3. Chop the noodles into 2-inch lengths and place in a medium-sized bowl.

4. In a small bowl, thoroughly combine the dressing ingredients and add to the noodles along with the carrots and watercress. Mix well.

5. Mound the noodle mixture in the center of a serving platter, and arrange the snow peas along the edge. Place a few broccoli florets on top of the mound, and arrange the rest along the edge. Serve immediately.

Summer Udon Salad

Whole grain udon noodles are combined with crunchy vegetables, and then tossed with a creamy miso-vinaigrette in this popular summer salad. Enjoy it as a satisfying meal or a delicious side dish—and vary the vegetable choices if you'd like.

1. In a 4-quart pot, bring 2 quarts of water to a rolling boil. Add the noodles and cook until al dente. Immediately drain the noodles and rinse under cold running water, or submerge in a bowl of cold water for 30 seconds or until cool. Drain and set aside.

2. In a pot of lightly salted water, parboil the broccoli and cauliflower for about 3 minutes, or until just tender-crisp. Transfer to a bowl of cold water to set the color and prevent further cooking. Drain and set aside.

3. Chop the noodles into 2-inch lengths and place in a medium-sized bowl along with the broccoli, cauliflower, cucumber, and scallion.

4. Whisk together the miso, vinegar, and water, and add to the noodle mixture. Toss gently, and serve.

Yield: 4 side-dish servings

8 ounces udon noodles

1 cup broccoli florets

1 cup cauliflower florets

1 small cucumber, peeled (if waxed), seeded, and sliced

1 scallion, finely minced

$1/3$ cup sweet or mellow miso

3 tablespoons brown rice vinegar

$1/4$ cup water

Spicy
Soba Salad

Yield: 3 servings

8 ounces soba noodles

1 large carrot, cut into
   matchsticks

1^1/$_2$ cups broccoli florets

2 scallions, slivered

2 tablespoons minced parsley

DRESSING

1 clove garlic, finely minced

3 tablespoons brown rice
   vinegar

2 tablespoons red or brown
   rice miso mixed with 2
   tablespoons water

1 tablespoon light sesame oil

1 tablespoon toasted
   sesame oil

^{1}/$_4$ teaspoon hot chili-
   flavored sesame oil

^{1}/$_4$ teaspoon sea salt

*Chili-flavored sesame oil adds a flavorful spark to this appetizing
noodle salad. Vary the vegetables according to their availability.
Fresh peas, corn, radishes, and red and green bell peppers are
colorful options.*

1. Break the noodles into 3 or 4 even lengths. In a 4-quart pot,
bring 2 quarts of water to a rolling boil. Add the noodles and
cook until al dente. Immediately drain the noodles and rinse
under cold running water, or submerge in a bowl of cold water
for 30 seconds or until cool. Drain and place in a medium-sized
bowl.

2. In a pot of lightly salted water, parboil the carrots for about
1 minute. Remove with a strainer and transfer to a bowl of cold
water to set the color and prevent further cooking. Drain and
add to the noodles.

3. Parboil the broccoli for about 3 minutes, or until just tender-
crisp, then transfer to the bowl of cold water. Drain and add to
the noodles.

4. Whisk together all of the dressing ingredients, and add to
the noodle mixture. Toss gently and serve.

Macaroni and Bean Salad

Great for potlucks and picnics, this simple, refreshing salad is perfect alongside fresh corn on the cob, grilled veggie burgers, and other summer favorites.

1. In a 4-quart pot, bring 2 quarts of water to a rolling boil. Add the salt and macaroni, stirring often until the water returns to a boil. Cook the macaroni until it is al dente, then drain and cool under cold running water. Drain again, and place in a medium-sized bowl.

2. In a pot of lightly salted water, parboil the beans for 3 to 5 minutes, or until bright green and tender-crisp. Transfer the beans to a bowl of cold water to set the color and prevent further cooking. Drain and add to the macaroni, along with the cucumber, scallions, radishes, chick peas, olives, and basil.

3. Add the dressing to the ingredients and toss well. Serve on individual lettuce-lined serving bowls.

**Yield: 4 to 6
side-dish servings**

1$\frac{1}{2}$ teaspoons sea salt

8 ounces ziti, shells, or other short-type macaroni

2 cups green beans, cut into 1-inch lengths

1 cucumber, peeled (if waxed), seeded, and sliced

5–6 scallions, thinly sliced

3 radishes, halved then sliced into half moons

1 cup cooked chick peas or red beans

$\frac{1}{3}$ cup sliced Kalamata olives, or chopped dill pickles

2 tablespoons minced fresh basil

$\frac{3}{4}$ cup Tahini-Herb Dressing (page 57)

Several whole lettuce leaves

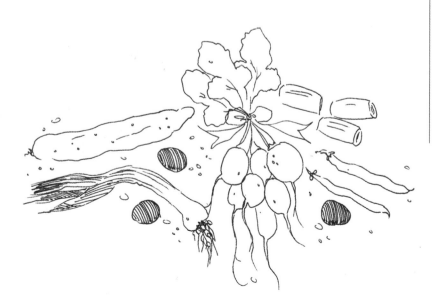

Macaroni Salad

Yield: 4 side-dish servings

8 ounces elbows or small
　shells

1$\frac{1}{2}$ teaspoons sea salt

1 medium cucumber, peeled
　(if waxed), quartered
　lengthwise, and sliced

$\frac{2}{3}$ cup diced green bell
　pepper

$\frac{1}{2}$ cup thinly sliced celery

$\frac{1}{2}$ cup thinly sliced radishes

$\frac{1}{2}$ cup minced scallion or
　red onion

$\frac{1}{4}$ cup minced parsley

DRESSING

$\frac{1}{4}$ cup water

3 tablespoons sweet or
　mellow miso

3 tablespoons tahini

2 tablespoons lemon juice

1 teaspoon ginger juice

Instead of high-fat mayonnaise, we use a lemony-ginger miso dressing for this flavorful pasta salad. In addition to tasting great, the dressing is nutritious and low in calories.

1. In a 4-quart pot, bring 2 quarts of water to a rolling boil. Add the salt and macaroni, stirring often until the water returns to a boil. Cook the macaroni until it is al dente, then drain and cool under cold running water. Drain again, and place in a large bowl.

2. Add the cucumber, bell pepper, celery, radishes, scallion, and parsley to the macaroni, and mix together.

3. Whisk together all of the dressing ingredients, and add to the macaroni mixture. Toss gently, and serve.

Pasta Primavera

Our dairy-free version of this colorful dish is rich and satisfying. Although you can vary the choice of vegetables, be careful not to overcook them. They should be tender-crisp.

1. In a pot of lightly salted water, parboil the vegetables individually until they are tender-crisp. Begin with the broccoli, letting it cook for about 3 minutes. Remove with a slotted spoon and transfer to a colander. Drain and place in a large bowl. Cook the carrots and corn for 2 to 3 minutes each. Drain and add to the broccoli.

2. In a 4-quart pot, bring 3 quarts of water a rolling boil to cook the macaroni.

3. While the water is coming to a boil, prepare the sauce. Heat the oil in a skillet over medium-low heat. Add the onion and garlic, and sauté for 2 minutes, or until the onion is just translucent.

4. Reduce the heat to low, and add the flour to the skillet, stirring constantly for 1 minute. Slowly add 1½ cups of the stock, continuing to stir until the sauce begins to thicken. Add a pinch of salt and pepper, and simmer 5 minutes. If the sauce is too thick, add a little more stock.

5. In a small bowl, combine the miso and tahini with the remaining stock. Add this mixture to the simmering sauce, and continue to gently simmer another minute. Stir in the vinegar, basil, and 3 tablespoons of the parsley. Keep the sauce warm but not boiling until you are ready to assemble the dish.

6. When the pot of water comes to a rolling boil, add the salt and cook the macaroni until it is al dente. Drain well and add to the vegetables. Top with the sauce and toss well.

7. Garnish with the remaining parsley and serve hot.

Yield: 4 servings

2 cups broccoli florets

2 cups carrots, cut into matchsticks

1 cup fresh corn kernels

2 teaspoons sea salt

12 ounces penne, shells, or other short-type macaroni

SAUCE

1½ tablespoons olive oil

1 small onion, diced

2 cloves garlic, finely minced

3 tablespoons unbleached white flour

1¾ cups Vegetable Stock (page 79)

Pinch salt

Pinch white pepper

2 tablespoons sweet or mellow miso

2 tablespoons tahini

1 tablespoon red wine vinegar or lemon juice

2 tablespoons finely chopped fresh basil

¼ cup minced parsley

Italian-Style Stuffed Shells

Yield: 4 to 6 servings

2 teaspoons sea salt

12 ounces large pasta shells

16 ounces prepared pasta sauce

Minced parsley for garnish

"RICOTTA" FILLING

1 pound firm tofu

4 cups fresh spinach, steamed for 1 minute and chopped

2 tablespoons tahini

1 tablespoon sweet or mellow miso

1 tablespoon minced garlic

1 tablespoon Italian seasoning

2 teaspoons umeboshi paste

Salt and pepper to taste

The American Miso Company contributed this popular recipe, which is always a hit with our family and friends. Sweet miso adds flavor and creaminess to the dairy-free filling.

1. Preheat the oven to 350°F.

2. In a 4-quart pot, bring 3 quarts of water a rolling boil. Add the salt and cook the shells halfway. Drain, rinse under cold water, and drain again.

3. While the shells are cooking, prepare the filling. Wrap the tofu in cheesecloth, muslin, or a clean kitchen towel, and gently squeeze out the excess water. Crumble the tofu into a medium-sized mixing bowl along with the spinach and the remaining filling ingredients. Mix well.

4. Spoon some sauce in the bottom of a medium-sized roasting pan or large baking dish. Fill the shells with the tofu mixture, and arrange them in the pan in a single layer. Top with the remaining sauce, cover, and bake for 25 minutes, or until the sauce is bubbling and shells are heated through.

5. Garnish with parsley before serving.

11. Grains and Beans

Grains and beans are the dietary heart and soul of most traditional societies. Beans and corn, for example, are the foundation of the Mexican diet; rice and soybean products, such as miso, tofu, and tempeh, have long sustained Asian cultures; and in northern Africa, millet, wheat, chick peas, and peanuts are culinary staples. Although agricultural developments have progressed at different times in different areas of the world, the practice of combining cooked grains and legumes for sustenance has been almost universally practiced since the dawn of civilization.

More recently, scientists have come to understand the wisdom of this traditional way of eating. Whole grains and beans each lack a number of essential amino acids and, therefore, do not provide complete protein when eaten alone. However, the amino acids that are missing in grains are abundant in beans, and vice versa. Thus, eating whole grains and beans together provides all the building blocks of protein the body needs.

Today, an extensive array of grains and beans is available, offering a wonderful diversity of color, taste, and texture to courses ranging from appetizers to desserts. The addition of miso provides extra flavor and nutritional value to these foods, while aiding in their digestion.

GRAINS

Whole grains are the mainstay of a healthy diet. With the amazing variety of delicious whole grains to choose from, we need never become bored with grain-centered meals. From old standbys like rice, corn, and wheat to exotic varieties like quinoa and teff, grains are used in breads and pastas, and can be featured in salads, soups, pilafs, breakfast foods, desserts, and a number of ethnic entrées. When served alone, basic whole grains can be elevated by the addition of a savory miso-enhanced sauce.

There are plenty of reasons to include grains in your daily meals. In addition to being relatively inexpensive, versatile, and easy to prepare, whole grains are nutritious. Rich in complex carbohydrates, fiber, vitamins, and minerals, they are also a good source of protein and low in fat. These attributes, particularly the abundance of fiber, are believed to be important in the prevention of some forms of cancer, heart disease, gallbladder problems, and a number of digestive ailments. Keep in mind, however, that these healthful qualities are lost or greatly reduced in grains that have been refined. The refining process removes the nutritional precious germ and outer fibrous layers. Eating refined grains, such as white rice and white flour, should be kept to a minimum.

With the exception of rice pilaf, we rarely add miso to grains as they cook. We do, however, serve millet, rice, buckwheat, barley and several other grains with a variety of miso-based sauces. Savory Brown Sauce (page 111), "Comfort" Gravy (page 112), and Fat-Free Shiitake Sauce (page 115) are just a few of our favorite choices for complementing simple boiled or pressure-cooked grains.

BEANS

Beans are back! Long held down by its image as "poor man's meat," the humble bean is gaining in culinary status. No longer background fare, beans are now featured in quality restaurants as well as kitchens across the country. They are tossed into salads—both simple and exotic—and used in a variety of dips, patés, and entrées.

It's no wonder bean popularity is on the rise. With some variation among different types of beans, a one-cup serving can supply 30 percent of the RDA of protein, as well as 15 percent of vitamin B and niacin, 40 percent of thiamine and folic acid, and 60 percent of iron. Beans are also a good source of calcium, riboflavin, phosphorus, magnesium, and zinc. Medical research has shown that they actually help lower serum cholesterol. As if that wasn't enough, beans are an excellent diet food, too. Very low in fat and high in fiber and carbohydrates, beans fill us quickly. Furthermore, since they digest slowly, beans satisfy us longer than most foods.

Two popular soybean products, tofu and tempeh, offer the benefits of soybeans plus some added advantages. They are easy to digest, versatile, and quick and easy to prepare. Tofu, for example, supplies complete protein

that is 90 percent digestible, and contains iron that is three times more available to our bodies than the iron in whole soybeans. Tempeh is a traditional Indonesian fermented whole soy food. As it is with most naturally fermented foods, the fermentation process enhances tempeh's overall nutritional value and digestibility.

One concern about whole beans is that they can be difficult to digest. Adding miso to whole beans as they cook—but only after they are tender—aids in their digestion. Along with adding miso, there is another way to increase the digestibility of whole beans—presoaking them. With the exception of azukis, lentils, and black-eyed peas, soak all beans prior to cooking. Either soak them in plenty of water for several hours or overnight, or bring one part beans and three parts water to a boil, simmer for two minutes, and remove from the heat. Allow the beans to soak for one or two hours, then drain them and cook in fresh water. A strip of kombu added to the cooking water is also believed to aid digestibility.

In general, miso goes very well with all types of beans and bean products. For hearty bean dishes, which are often used to replace meat in vegetarian cuisine, dark, long-aged misos are typically preferred. In dishes such as Tofu Lasagna (page 154), the dairy-like quality of sweet, light miso is called for. You will find beans or bean products featured in a number of soup, salad, dip, and pasta recipes in other chapters of this book.

Enjoy the following recipes, which pair miso with a variety of bean and grain dishes. Hopefully, they will encourage you to include miso in your own favorite recipes for these staple foods.

Boston Baked Beans

One of our favorite winter meals includes Boston baked beans served with cornbread and a side of greens. Comforting, nutritious, and flavorful, it makes us feel strong and balanced.

1. Cover the beans with plenty of water and soak for 6 to 10 hours, or bring to a boil with 6 cups water, simmer 2 minutes, and soak for 1 to 2 hours.

2. Drain the beans and place in a 4-quart pot along with 8 cups fresh water. Bring to a boil, cover, and reduce the heat to low. Simmer for $1\frac{1}{2}$ to 2 hours or until tender.

3. Add the salt and simmer 15 minutes more. Drain the beans, reserving the broth, and set aside.

4. Preheat the oven to 325°F.

5. Heat the oil in a 3-quart pot over medium heat. Add the onions and sauté for 3 to 5 minutes, or until they are soft and translucent.

6. Combine the miso and molasses with $1\frac{1}{4}$ cups of the reserved bean broth, and add to the pot along with the mustard, pepper, and drained beans.

7. Bring the mixture to a simmer, and then transfer to a 2-quart bean pot or casserole dish.

8. Bake uncovered for $1\frac{1}{2}$ hours, stirring every 20 minutes and adding more broth if necessary.

9. Serve hot. Refrigerate any leftovers for up to 5 days.

Yield: 6 servings

2 cups dried navy beans

8 cups water

$\frac{1}{2}$ teaspoon sea salt

2 tablespoons vegetable oil

$1\frac{1}{2}$ cups diced onion

3 tablespoons rice or barley miso

$\frac{1}{4}$ cup molasses

2 teaspoons dry mustard

$\frac{1}{2}$ teaspoon white or black pepper

Refried Beans

Yield: 2½ cups

1 cup dried pinto or black turtle beans

4 cups water

1 teaspoon sea salt

2 tablespoons extra-virgin olive oil

1 onion, diced

3–4 cloves garlic, minced

⅓ cup diced green bell pepper

½ teaspoon shoyu

1 tablespoon rice or barley miso

1 tablespoon lemon juice

Refried beans are a tasty filling for tacos, chapattis, and burritos. Although most standard recipes call for hot peppers and cheese, this version uses lemon juice for a light delicious flavor. If you like a spicier taste, add a little hot sauce or salsa to the mixture.

1. Cover the beans with plenty of water and soak for 6 to 10 hours, or bring to a boil with 3 cups water, simmer 2 minutes, and soak 1 to 2 hours.

2. Drain the beans and place in a 2-quart pot along with 4 cups fresh water. Bring to a boil, cover, and reduce the heat to low. Simmer for 1½ to 2 hours, or until tender.

3. Add the salt and simmer 15 to 20 minutes more. Drain the beans, reserving the broth, and set aside.

4. Heat the oil in a skillet over medium heat. Add the onion, garlic, and green pepper, and sauté for 3 to 5 minutes, or until the onions are soft and translucent.

5. Add the beans, and sauté 2 to 3 minutes. Stir in the shoyu and ⅓ cup of the reserved bean broth, and partially mash the beans. Combine the miso and lemon juice, and add to the bean mixture. Add more broth if the mixture is too dry. Cook 1 minute more.

6. Serve immediately.

Beans & Cornbread Casserole

This recipe borrows from two old favorites—tamale pie and chili—only our version is meatless and tomato-less. The cornbread is baked right on top.

1. Cover the beans with plenty of water and soak for 6 to 10 hours, or bring to a boil with 3 cups of water, simmer 2 minutes, and soak 1 to 2 hours.

2. Drain the beans and place in a pressure cooker with 5 cups fresh water and kombu, if using. Cover and bring to pressure, reduce the heat, and cook 50 to 60 minutes.

3. Allow the pressure to return to normal. Add the salt, bay leaf, cayenne pepper, cumin, garlic, onion, carrot, bell peppers, and celery. Simmer uncovered for 10 minutes. The mixture should be thick like chili, but not dry.

4. Preheat the oven to 425°F.

5. Stir the miso into the bean mixture, then pour the mixture into a 3-quart casserole. Set aside.

6. To prepare the cornbread topping, combine the cornmeal, flour, salt, and baking powder in a medium-sized bowl. Set aside.

7. In a small bowl, whisk together the egg, if using, along with the syrup, water, and oil. Add to the cornmeal mixture and stir until just blended. Do not overstir.

8. Spoon the batter over the bean mixture. (It will partially sink into the beans, but will rise as it bakes.)

9. Bake uncovered for 20 to 25 minutes, or until the cornbread crust is firm and golden. Serve hot.

Yield: 4 to 5 servings

2 cups pinto beans

5 cups water

3-inch piece kombu (optional)

$1\frac{1}{2}$ teaspoons sea salt

1 bay leaf

$\frac{1}{4}$ teaspoon cayenne pepper

1 teaspoon cumin

2 cloves garlic, minced

1 large onion, diced

1 large carrot, diced

1 cup diced bell peppers

1 rib celery, sliced

1 tablespoon red or barley miso mixed with 1 tablespoon water

CORNBREAD

1 cup yellow cornmeal

2 tablespoons whole wheat flour

$\frac{1}{4}$ teaspoon sea salt

$1\frac{1}{2}$ teaspoons baking powder

1 egg, lightly beaten (optional)

2 tablespoons rice or maple syrup

$\frac{1}{2}$–$\frac{2}{3}$ cup water (use greater amount if omitting egg)

1 tablespoon corn or other vegetable oil

Tempeh Bourguignon

Yield: 3 servings

8 ounces tempeh

1³/₄ cups dry red wine

1 teaspoon tamari or shoyu

2 tablespoons red or barley
  miso mixed with 2
  tablespoons water

¹/₄ teaspoon dried thyme

¹/₄ teaspoon black or white
  pepper

1 large clove garlic, sliced

2 tablespoons extra-virgin
  olive oil

2 tablespoons arrowroot
  powder

1 cup water or vegetable
  stock

1 bay leaf

2 pinches sea salt

20 pearl onions

10 medium button
  mushrooms, cut into pie-
  shaped wedges

¹/₄ cup chopped parsley

Rich in flavor, this delicious entrée is a good choice when you're having guests for dinner. We usually serve it over noodles, but enjoy it plain as well. Although the recipe is a little complex, it's well worth the effort.

1. Cut the tempeh into two slabs (about ¹/₃-inch thick), then dice into ³/₄-inch squares. Place the tempeh in a vegetable steamer set over boiling water and steam for 30 minutes.

2. In a medium-sized bowl, combine 1¹/₄ cups of the wine with the tamari, miso, thyme, pepper, and garlic. Stir to dissolve the miso. Add the steamed tempeh and let marinate for 8 to 24 hours. Place a small plate on the tempeh to keep it submerged.

3. Drain the tempeh, reserving the marinade and discarding the garlic.

4. Heat 1¹/₂ tablespoons of the oil in a large skillet over medium heat. Add the tempeh and brown on both sides.

5. Remove the skillet from the heat, sprinkle the tempeh with arrowroot, and toss gently to coat evenly. Cover with the reserved marinade, water, and remaining wine. Stir well.

6. Transfer the ingredients to a 2-quart pot set over medium-low heat and bring to a simmer. Add the bay leaf and a pinch of salt, cover, and gently simmer for 45 minutes.

7. While the tempeh is cooking, blanch the unpeeled onions in 2 cups of boiling water for 3 minutes. After draining the onions, trim away the root ends, and then squeeze the tips to remove the outer peel. Cut off any tough, fibrous tips.

8. After the tempeh has simmered for 45 minutes, add the onions. Simmer another 30 minutes, stirring occasionally and adding more water or stock as needed.

9. Heat the remaining oil in a medium-sized skillet over medium heat. Add the mushrooms along with a pinch of salt and pepper. Sauté 4 to 5 minutes, or until the mushrooms are tender. If the pan becomes dry, add 1 to 2 teaspoons of water or wine.

10. Fold the mushrooms into the stew along with another pinch of pepper and thyme. Simmer 5 minutes more, adding 3 tablespoons of the parsley during the last minute of cooking.

11. Spoon the hot stew into bowls either as is or over a bed of noodles. Garnish with the remaining parsley and serve.

Instant Tofu "Cheese"

Low in calories, nutritious and flavorful, this instant version of tofu "cheese" is similar to ricotta. It is a satisfying substitute for cheese in dairy-free versions of other Italian favorites like baked ziti and Tofu Lasagna (page 154). We also add it to bread crumbs as an "au gratin" topping for vegetable and noodle casseroles.

Yield: About 2 cups

1 pound firm fresh tofu

3 level tablespoons mellow white miso mixed with 2 tablespoons water

2 tablespoons tahini

1 clove garlic, finely minced

2 teaspoons lemon juice or brown rice vinegar

3 tablespoons chopped parsley

1 egg, beaten

1. Wrap the tofu in a clean dry towel and gently squeeze to remove any excess water.

2. Crumble the tofu into a medium-sized bowl and mash with a fork or potato masher.

3. Combine the miso and tahini, and add to the tofu. Mix well. Stir in the garlic, lemon juice, and parsley, then fold in the beaten egg.

4. Use this "cheese" immediately, or refrigerate and use within a few hours.

Tofu Lasagna

Yield: 6 servings

8 lasagna noodles

2 teaspoons olive oil

2 cloves garlic, minced

5–6 button mushrooms, sliced

Pinch sea salt

3¹/₂ cups spaghetti sauce

¹/₃ teaspoon dried oregano or marjoram

¹/₄ teaspoon dried thyme

2 cups Instant Tofu "Cheese" (page 153)

This simple, dairy-free version of one of America's favorite ethnic entrées is quick and easy to make. Serve it with a salad and garlic toast for a delicious, satisfying meal.

1. Bring a 3-quart pot of salted water to a rapid boil, and cook the noodles according to package directions. They should be a little underdone (*al dente*). Drain the noodles, place in a bowl of cold water, and set aside.

2. Heat the oil in a large skillet over medium-low heat. Add the garlic, mushrooms, and salt, and sauté for 2 to 3 minutes, or until the mushrooms begin to soften.

3. Add the spaghetti sauce and bring to a simmer. Stir in the oregano and thyme, and simmer another 2 to 3 minutes.

4. Preheat the oven to 350°F.

5. To assemble the lasagna, spoon a little sauce on the bottom of a 9¹/₂-x-13-inch baking pan. Drain the noodles and cover the bottom of the pan with half, overlapping them slightly where the edges meet. Spread half of the "cheese" evenly over the noodles, and top with half of the sauce. Repeat the layers.

6. Bake uncovered for 30 to 40 minutes, or until heated through. Remove from the oven and allow to sit for 10 minutes before serving.

Truckstop Chili

This tasty vegetarian version of the popular Southwestern dish is a good choice to serve guests who are not accustomed to meatless cooking. They'll never know the difference; so don't give away your secret until they've tried it.

1. Cover the beans with plenty of water and soak for 6 to 10 hours, or bring to a boil with 3 cups of water, simmer 2 minutes, and soak 1 to 2 hours.

2. Drain the beans and place them in a 2-quart pot along with 4 cups fresh water. Bring to a boil, cover, and reduce the heat to low. Simmer for $1\frac{1}{2}$ to 2 hours, or until the beans are nearly tender.

3. Heat the oil in a large skillet over medium-low heat. Add the garlic and onion, and sauté for 2 to 3 minutes, or until the onion is soft and translucent.

4. Add the green pepper and continue to sauté for 2 to 3 minutes. Stir in the seitan, cumin, chili powder, and black pepper, and sauté a few minutes more.

5. When the beans are tender, add the seitan mixture, miso, bay leaf, tomato paste, and corn, if using. The chili should be thick but not dry. If necessary, add a little more water. Bring the ingredients to a simmer, add the cayenne pepper, if using, and continue to simmer for 10 to 15 minutes.

6. Stir in the oregano and paprika, cook another minute or two, and serve hot.

Yield: 6 servings

1 cup dried pinto beans

4 cups water

1 tablespoon extra-virgin olive oil

4 cloves garlic, minced

1 onion, diced

1 green pepper, coarsely chopped

2 cups seitan ("wheat meat"), minced or coarsely ground

2 teaspoons cumin powder

2–3 teaspoons chili powder

$\frac{1}{4}$ teaspoon black pepper

$2\frac{1}{2}$ tablespoons red or barley miso mixed with 2 tablespoons water

1 bay leaf

4 ounces tomato paste mixed with $\frac{1}{4}$ cup water

1 cup fresh or frozen corn kernels (optional)

$\frac{1}{2}$ teaspoon cayenne pepper (optional)

1 teaspoon dried oregano

2 teaspoons paprika

Barley-Corn Confetti Salad

Yield: 4 servings

1 cup barley

6 cups water

$^1/_4$ teaspoon sea salt

2 cups cooked corn kernels

$^1/_2$ cup thinly sliced scallion

1 red bell pepper, seeded and diced

$^1/_2$ cup chopped parsley

Mustard Vinaigrette (page 61), or Oil and Vinegar Dressing (page 62)

A wholesome, easily digested grain with a sweet taste and chewy substantial texture, barley is an excellent choice for a grain salad.

1. Rinse and drain the barley 3 or 4 times, or until the rinse water is almost clear.

2. Bring the water and salt to a boil in a 3-quart pot. Add the barley, cover, and reduce the heat to low. Simmer for 40 minutes, or until just tender.

3. Transfer the barley to a colander, rinse under cold water, and drain well.

4. Place the barley, corn, scallion, bell pepper, and parsley in a medium-sized bowl and toss.

5. Drizzle the dressing over the mixture, toss again, and serve.

Rice Burgers

Our friend Kaoru Onozaki showed us this delicious way to use leftover rice.

1. Coarsely grind the sesame seeds in a suribachi or mortar.

2. In a medium-sized mixing bowl, cut the miso into the rice with the side of a wooden spoon or rice paddle. Add the scallion, parsley, carrot, and sesame seeds, and mix well. Add the flour a little at a time until the mixture is fairly dry (not too sticky) and holds its shape well.

3. Moisten your hands with a little water or vegetable oil, and form the mixture into six patties. If the patties are sticky, lightly dust both sides with flour before cooking.

4. Heat the oil in a large skillet over low heat. Add the patties, cover, and cook until the bottoms are golden brown. Flip the patties over and cook until browned on the second side.

5. Serve as is, or topped with a light spread of butter or non-hydrogenated vegetable margarine and a sprinkling of shoyu.

Yield: 6 burgers (3-inch)

3 tablespoons toasted sesame seeds

2$\frac{1}{2}$ cups cooked white or brown rice

3 level tablespoons sweet or mellow miso mixed with 2 tablespoons water

$\frac{1}{3}$ cup minced scallion

$\frac{1}{3}$ cup minced parsley

$\frac{2}{3}$ cup grated carrot

$\frac{1}{4}$ cup whole wheat or unbleached white flour

1 tablespoon light sesame or safflower oil

Rice Pilaf

Yield: 6 servings

4 cups water

3 dried shiitake mushrooms

4-inch piece kombu
  (optional)

3 cups brown rice, washed
  and drained

$1/4$ cup rice or barley miso

$1/3$ cup minced onion

$1/3$ cup minced celery

1 bay leaf

$2/3$ cup minced parsley

Flavorful and nutritious, this basic rice dish is an excellent way to serve brown rice. Turn any leftovers into delicious fried rice.

1. Place the water in a pressure cooker, add the shiitake, and let soak for 20 to 30 minutes. Add the kombu, if using, and bring to a simmer, uncovered, over medium heat for 5 minutes. Remove the kombu and reserve for another use.

2. Remove the shiitake and discard the stems. Mince the caps and return to the stock.

3. Place the rice in an unoiled skillet over medium heat. Stirring constantly, toast the grains for about 5 minutes, or until golden and fragrant.

4. Dissolve the miso in a little of the stock, and add to the pressure cooker along with the onion, celery, and bay leaf.

5. Bring to a boil and slowly add the toasted rice. Boil for 1 minute, then cover, bring to pressure, and cook 45 minutes.

6. Remove from the heat and allow pressure to return to normal. Uncover, add the parsley, and toss well. Cover and let sit for 10 minutes.

7. Garnish with a sprig of parsley and serve.

Note: If cooking on the stovetop, use a heavy 3-quart pot with a tight-fitting lid. Increase the water to 6 cups, and add an extra tablespoon of miso. After the ingredients have been brought to a boil, reduce the heat to medium-low and simmer for 40 minutes. Then reduce the heat to its lowest setting and cook 20 minutes more. Do not remove the cover while cooking.

Wild Rice Pilaf

Wild rice has a delicious, nutty flavor that is perfect in pilafs. To be economical, we use a blend of long grain brown rice and wild rice, which is available in most natural foods stores, gourmet shops, and large supermarkets.

1. Heat the oil in a large skillet over medium heat. Add the garlic and onion, and sauté for about 2 minutes, or until the onion is soft and translucent.

2. Add the bell pepper, mushrooms, and salt, and continue to sauté for 2 to 3 minutes, or until the mushrooms begin to soften. Add the rice and toss to coat evenly.

3. Stir the stock and miso into the skillet, add the bay leaf, and bring to a boil. Reduce the heat to low, cover, and simmer for 50 minutes, or until all of the liquid is absorbed.

4. Remove from heat and mix in most of the parsley, reserving a little for garnish. Cover and let sit 5 to 10 minutes.

5. Garnish with the remaining parsley and some of the almonds. Place the rest of the almonds in a bowl and use as a condiment.

Yield: 4 servings

1 tablespoon olive oil

2 cloves garlic, minced

1 medium onion, diced

$1/3$ cup diced green or red bell pepper

6 crimini or shiitake mushroom caps, chopped

Pinch sea salt

2 cups brown/wild rice blend, washed and drained

4 cups Vegetable Stock (page 79)

3 tablespoons red or barley miso mixed with 3 tablespoons water

1 bay leaf

$1/3$ cup minced parsley

$1/2$ cup toasted slivered almonds

Peanutty Crisped Rice Treats

Yield: 16 treats (2-inch squares)

$1/2$ cup unsalted peanut butter

Scant $1/2$ cup rice syrup

2 teaspoons sweet white miso mixed with 2 teaspoons water

$1/2$ teaspoon vanilla

$1/4$ teaspoon cinnamon

$1/4$ cup nondairy chocolate chips

$1/4$ cup shredded coconut

$2^1/2$ cups crispy brown rice cereal*

*Erewhon brand "Rice Twice" Crisped Brown Rice Cereal is recommended.

This easy-to-make dessert has a satisfying crunch, and makes a perfect lunchbox treat or nutritious between-meal snack.

1. Preheat the oven to 350°F.

2. Combine the peanut butter, rice syrup, miso, vanilla, and cinnamon in a medium-sized bowl. Stir in the chocolate chips and coconut.

3. Add the cereal and gently toss until evenly coated.

4. Press the mixture into an unoiled 8-inch-square baking pan. Bake for 12 to 15 minutes or until the edges are lightly browned. Allow to cool on a wire rack.

5. Cut into 2-inch squares and serve.

Almond Crisped Rice Treats

Yield: 16 treats (2-inch squares)

$1/2$ cup unsalted almond butter

Scant $1/2$ cup rice syrup

2 teaspoons sweet white miso mixed with 2 teaspoons water

$1/2$ teaspoon vanilla extract

$1/8$ teaspoon almond extract

$2^1/2$ cups crispy brown rice cereal*

*Erewhon brand "Rice Twice" Crisped Brown Rice Cereal is recommended.

Almond butter gives these bars an especially rich, satisfying flavor.

1. Preheat the oven to 350°F.

2. Combine the almond butter, rice syrup, miso, vanilla, and almond extract in a medium-sized bowl and mix well.

3. Add the cereal and gently toss until evenly coated.

4. Press the mixture into an unoiled 8-inch-square baking pan. Bake for 12 to 15 minutes or until the edges are lightly browned. Allow to cool on a wire rack.

5. Cut into 2-inch squares and serve.

Apple-Nut Muffins

Miso is an excellent substitute for salt in many recipes. It supplies more flavor and nutrition than plain salt. In this recipe, 2 tablespoons of mellow miso replace $1/2$ teaspoon of sea salt.

1. Preheat the oven to 400°F.

2. Whisk together the oil and rice syrup in a large mixing bowl. Mix in the egg, if using. Add the miso and tahini, and whisk vigorously until smooth. Stir in the apple juice and water.

3. Place the flour, cinnamon, baking soda, and baking powder in a medium-sized bowl, and stir until well combined.

4. Add the dry mixture to the liquid mixture, and stir gently with a wooden spoon until just mixed. Do not overstir. Fold in the apples, walnuts, and raisins.

5. Spoon the batter into oiled or papered muffin tins. Fill each cup about seven-eighths full.

6. Bake for 20 to 25 minutes, or until the tops of the muffins spring back when lightly pressed. Allow to cool for 10 minutes in the tin, then remove the muffins and cool completely on a wire rack.

7. Serve immediately, or store in an airtight container for up to a week.

Yield: 12 muffins

$1/4$ cup vegetable oil

$1/3$ cup rice syrup, or $1/4$ cup maple syrup

1 egg (optional)

2 tablespoons sweet or mellow miso

2 tablespoons tahini (optional)

1 cup apple juice

$3/4$ cup water

$2 1/4$ cups whole wheat pastry flour

1 teaspoon cinnamon

1 teaspoon baking soda

$1/4$ teaspoon baking powder

$1/2$ cup chopped dried apples

$1/2$ cup chopped walnuts

$1/3$ cup raisins

12. Seafood Entrées

With the variety of available seafood and its versatility in cooking, there's a delicious fish dish for every taste and occasion. In the mood for a hearty, robust entrée? Broiled Salmon Steaks (page 169) will deliver with ease. Want something more delicate? Your taste buds will delight in succulent Marinated Steamed White Fish Fillets (page 171) or Orange Roughy with Citrus Vinaigrette (page 165). Having special guests for dinner? Impress them with Broiled Catch of the Day with Salsa Verde (page 166). As an added bonus, these and most other fish dishes are quick and easy to prepare.

There are far more reasons to enjoy seafood than simply its flavor, ease of preparation, and versatility. Seafood has long been touted for its nutritional profile and health benefits. It is an excellent source of protein, B vitamins (including B_{12}), and minerals. Most types are low in saturated fat and cholesterol, and many are rich in essential omega-3 fatty acids. Omega 3s offer numerous health benefits, including the ability to lower triglyceride levels, important for a healthy heart. Studies have shown that as little as one large or two small portions of seafood per week can significantly reduce the risk of heart disease.

Miso goes very well with fish and seafood. In marinades, it is a wonderful tenderizing agent. When used in place of salt in sauces and other toppings, it contributes both flavor and healthful benefits. For delicate fish dishes like Lemon-Mustard Broiled Flounder (page 168), we generally use sweet or mellow white miso. Darker misos are better suited for enhancing robust sauces, such as the one used with Szechuan Shrimp (page 173).

With some basic knowledge of how to choose and prepare fish, you can easily develop a varied repertoire of exciting seafood dishes and reap the benefits they offer. The key to success always begins with freshness. For freshness guidelines, see "Fresh Catch of the Day" on pages 168 and 169.

Reports about water pollution and contaminants in seafood may have you wondering about its safety. Most fish are safe and deserving of their healthful reputation; however, when shopping for fish, it's important to be aware of which varieties are recommended and which should be avoided or eaten sparingly.

Problems center around seafood that comes from polluted coastal waters, especially those close to industrial centers. Shellfish are particularly prone to bacteria and pollutants. Be sure to purchase them from a fish dealer who can vouch for their source. And avoid eating oysters, clams, and other fish raw.

Warnings have recently been issued about farm-raised salmon because analysis has indicated that it contains significantly more dioxins, polychlorinated biphenyls (PCBs), and other pollutants than wild salmon. The pollutant levels vary depending on their origin—salmon farmed in Northern Europe contains the greatest number of contaminants, followed by North America and Chile. Farm-raised salmon from Chile is the closest to wild salmon in terms of contaminant levels, and it is the type sold primarily in the United States. Wild salmon is also seasonal. When it is unavailable, we recommend buying farm-raised salmon only if it was raised in Chile.

Most commercially caught seafood comes from deep waters, far from polluted shores. Among deep ocean varieties, large, fatty predatory fish, such as bluefish, striped bass, swordfish, tuna, and shark, tend to accumulate toxins in their fat. Before eating these varieties, always trim away the skin, the belly flaps of steaks, and any fatty portions, which include dark red areas of flesh. Small to medium-sized low-fat fish, such as scrod and cod, sole, flounder, pollock, orange roughy, turbot, ocean perch, haddock, and mahi-mahi are considered safest.

If you buy frozen fish, be aware that some merchants freeze fish that is past its prime in an attempt to extend its shelf life. To avoid this, look for the words "fresh-frozen," the term for fish that is frozen shortly after being caught. Don't be fooled by labels that boast the frozen fish to be "fancy." Although this may sound attractive, it is an industry term for "previously frozen."

When cooking fish, keep in mind that it is fragile. To help keep it from falling apart, handle it as little as possible, turning it no more than once. And leave the skin on fillets and steaks during the cooking process. To prevent fillets from curling, make a few shallow diagonal slashes across the skin. To ensure even cooking, tuck any thin ends under. And be careful not to overcook the fish, which is a common mistake. In a matter of minutes, a piece of fish can go from tender and succulent to dry and uninteresting. Fish is ready when the flesh is opaque and flakes easily with a fork.

Miso is used as a seasoning and tenderizer, adding flavor and interest to a variety of seafood dishes in this chapter. Whether you are looking for a quick and easy entrée that you can feel good about serving to your family, or a dish for a special occasion, you are sure to find it here.

Orange Roughy with Citrus Vinaigrette

Orange roughy's mild-flavored, tender white flesh is enhanced by a simple but zesty golden vinaigrette in this dish, which was created years ago by John Belleme, Jr. Eye appealing and delicious, it remains one of our favorites.

1. Preheat the oven to 400°F. Lightly oil a medium-sized baking dish and set aside.

2. Whisk together the vinaigrette ingredients in a small bowl and set aside.

3. Bring 1 to 2 cups of water to boil in a 1-quart saucepan, add a pinch of salt and the green beans. When the water returns to a boil, add the carrots. Reduce the heat to low, and simmer uncovered for 3 minutes, or until the vegetables are bright in color and tender-crisp. Drain immediately and rinse under cold water to set the color. Drain and set aside.

4. Rinse the fish and pat dry. Season lightly with salt and pepper, and arrange in the baking dish. Cover tightly with aluminum foil, and bake for 10 minutes, or until the fish is opaque and can be easily flaked with a fork.

5. Transfer the cooked fish to a platter, and spoon half the vinaigrette on top. Top with green beans, carrots, and scallion. Spoon the remaining vinaigrette on top and serve.

Yield: 4 servings

3–4 green beans, thinly sliced on the diagonal (French style)

1 small carrot, cut into matchsticks

$1\frac{1}{3}$ pounds orange roughy fillets

Pinch sea salt

Pinch white or black pepper

1 scallion, thinly sliced on the diagonal

CITRUS VINAIGRETTE

2 tablespoons lemon juice

2 tablespoons extra-virgin olive oil

1 tablespoon orange juice

1 tablespoon sweet or mellow white miso

$1\frac{1}{2}$ teaspoons finely grated lemon rind

1 teaspoon prepared stone-ground mustard

Pinch white or black pepper

Broiled Catch of the Day with Salsa Verde

Yield: 4 servings

1½ pounds salmon, grouper, snapper, or other firm-textured fish

Olive oil for basting

Pinch sea salt

Pinch white or black pepper

SALSA VERDE

3 tablespoons finely chopped fresh basil

1½ tablespoons finely chopped fresh parsley

1 tablespoon finely minced red or white onion

1 tablespoon finely minced toasted pine nuts

2 teaspoons sweet or mellow white miso mixed with 2 teaspoons water

1 rounded teaspoon finely minced garlic

1 teaspoon lemon juice

½ tablespoon extra-virgin olive oil

Another outstanding creation by John Belleme, Jr., this recipe is actually more about the sauce than the fish. This version of Salsa Verde or "green sauce" combines the fresh taste of herbs with miso and the incomparable flavor of extra-virgin olive oil. It brings out the best in seafood steaks or firm-textured fillets such as salmon, grouper, and snapper.

1. Preheat the broiler. Lightly oil a baking sheet and set aside.

2. Combine all of the Salsa Verde ingredients except the oil in a small bowl, and stir until evenly mixed. Stir in the oil and mix well. The consistency should be similar to pesto or a bit thinner. Set aside.

3. Rinse the fish and pat dry. If cooking fillets with skin, make a few shallow, diagonal slashes in the skin to prevent curling.

4. Arrange the fish in a single layer on the baking sheet. If using fillets with skin, place them flesh side down. If they taper to very thin ends, fold the ends under so the fish cooks evenly. Brush the tops with olive oil and sprinkle lightly with salt and pepper.

5. Cook about 8 to 9 minutes per inch of thickness. When half cooked, turn the fish over, baste with olive oil, and continue to cook until opaque and easily flaked with a fork.

6. Transfer the fish to a serving platter. Top with Salsa Verde and serve immediately.

Swordfish with Basil-Miso Sauce

Succulent swordfish steaks are crowned with a garlicky basil-miso sauce in this delectable cold-weather entrée.

1. In a small pot of boiling water, add the carrots and cook for 2 minutes, or until just tender. Drain and place in a small bowl.

2. In the same pot, bring $1\frac{1}{3}$ cups water to a simmer. Remove from the heat, add the miso and shoyu, and stir until the miso is dissolved. Set aside.

3. Rinse the salmon steaks and pat dry.

4. Heat the oil in a large skillet over medium heat. Add the steaks and cook for 3 minutes. Turn over and cook another 2 to 3 minutes. Transfer the steaks to a heatproof platter and keep warm in a 225°F oven. The fish will be rare, but will finish cooking in the oven.

5. Stirring constantly, add the flour to the pan drippings and cook for 2 minutes over medium-low heat. While continuing to stir, add the shallots and garlic, and sauté for 1 minute before adding the wine and miso mixture. Simmer while stirring frequently until the sauce is smooth.

6. Reduce the heat to low, add the basil and lemon juice, and simmer for 5 minutes, or until the sauce is thick and the floury taste is gone.

7. Stir in the scallions and carrots, cook 1 minute more, and remove from heat.

8. Spoon the sauce over the fish and serve immediately.

Yield: 4 servings

$2/3$ cup julienned carrots

$1\frac{1}{3}$ cups water

2 level tablespoons red, brown rice, or barley miso

$1/2$ teaspoon shoyu or tamari

4 swordfish or salmon steaks ($3/4$-inch thick)

5 tablespoons safflower oil

$2\frac{1}{2}$ tablespoons unbleached white flour

2 shallots, minced

1 clove garlic, finely minced

$2/3$ cup dry white wine

3 tablespoons chopped fresh basil leaves

$2\frac{1}{2}$ teaspoons lemon juice

3 scallions, thinly sliced on the diagonal

Lemon–Mustard Broiled Flounder

Yield: 4 servings

3 tablespoons lemon juice

2 tablespoons sweet or mellow white miso

1 tablespoon stone-ground mustard

1 tablespoon extra-virgin olive oil

$1/4$ teaspoon black pepper (optional)

4 flounder fillets (4 ounces each)

4 lemon wedges

This tasty entrée takes only ten minutes to prepare. When combined with steamed vegetables and whole grain rolls, it provides a healthy, complete meal.

1. Preheat the broiler. Lightly oil a baking sheet and set aside.

2. Combine the lemon juice, miso, mustard, olive oil, and pepper, if using, in a small bowl.

3. Rinse the flounder and pat dry. Arrange the fillets on the baking sheet and spoon half of the sauce evenly over the tops. Broil for 3 to 4 minutes, or until the fish is opaque and can be easily flaked with a fork. Do not turn.

4. Transfer the fillets to a serving platter, top with the remaining sauce, and serve with lemon wedges.

Fresh Catch of the Day

Fish is highly perishable, so it is important to buy and store it properly. To make sure your catch is fresh and tasty, keep the following guidelines in mind:

☐ Use your eyes. Fish should look tempting. If buying fish whole, select those with eyes that are bright and clear, not cloudy or sunken. The scales should be tightly packed and shiny, and the flesh should be firm and spring back when touched. Look for gills that are red or bright pink, rather than brown and dull. Finally, check the tail. If it's dried out, the fish is probably not fresh. When buying fish fillets and steaks, make sure they are dense and firm with flesh that is translucent, not opaque.

☐ Use your nose. Don't rely on your eyes alone. Smelling fish is the surest test of freshness. Fresh fish has a pleasant, mild scent that should be fresh and clean, never "fishy." There should be no hint of ammonia or other off odor.

☐ Whenever possible, buy fish from a busy, reliable fish store. (The faster the turnover rate, the fresher the fish is likely to be.) The fish should be displayed on ice, which helps maintain freshness, and the

Broiled Salmon Steaks

Swordfish can be substituted for the salmon in this simple entrée with equally delicious results.

1. Preheat the broiler. Lightly oil a baking sheet and set aside.

2. Combine the olive oil, wine, miso/lemon mixture, garlic powder, and basil in a small bowl.

3. Rinse the salmon steaks and pat dry. Arrange the steaks on the baking sheet and brush the tops with the olive oil mixture. Broil 5 minutes, baste again, then turn the steaks over. Baste the tops and continue to broil another 4 to 5 minutes, or just until the fish is opaque and can be easily flaked with a fork.

4. Bring the remaining sauce to a slow simmer over medium-low heat for 1 minute.

5. Transfer the steaks to a serving platter, top with sauce, and serve immediately.

Yield: 2 servings

3 tablespoons olive oil

2 tablespoons white wine or sake

2 tablespoons sweet or mellow white miso mixed with 2 tablespoons lemon juice

Pinch garlic powder

$1/4$ teaspoon dried basil or 2 teaspoons fresh basil, minced

2 salmon steaks

---

counters should be clean. Although it's best to avoid buying packaged fish, when you have no other choice, be sure to inspect the package to make sure that it contains no visible liquid, which, along with the packaging material, promotes bacterial growth.

☐ When purchasing shrimp, keep in mind that, depending on the variety, shrimp can be light gray, brownish pink, or red when raw. For this reason, don't use color as an indication of freshness. Do, however, choose shrimp that are dry and firm. When selecting unshelled varieties, look for those with shiny shells.

☐ When buying shellfish, such as clams and mussels, make sure the shells are firmly closed. Avoid those that are strong smelling.

☐ Choose scallops that are firm, free of cloudy liquid, and sweet smelling. An ammonia or sulfur-like odor is a clear sign that the scallops are not fresh.

☐ As soon as you get your fish home, place it in the coldest part of the refrigerator (but not the freezer), and keep it there until you're ready to prepare it. Whenever possible, use fresh fish within twenty-four hours of purchase.

Shrimp Japonais

Yield: 4 servings

1 pound large or jumbo shrimp

Ginger-Miso Marinade (page 119)

2¹/₂ tablespoons light sesame or safflower oil

1 large onion, halved lengthwise and thinly sliced

3¹/₂ cups sliced mushrooms

1–2 cloves garlic, finely minced

2 tablespoons sake or dry white wine

3 scallions, thinly sliced on the diagonal

Here's a main course that's a snap to prepare, yet special enough to serve guests. We usually enjoy it with a simple clear soup, blanched broccoli or green beans, and rice.

1. Peel and devein the shrimp, leaving the tail. Place the shrimp in a medium-sized bowl, add the marinade, and toss to coat. Let marinate in the refrigerator for 45 to 60 minutes, stirring occasionally.

2. Heat the oil in a wok or skillet over medium-high heat. Remove the shrimp from the marinade, toss in the wok, and sauté for 2 minutes, or until just pink. Remove from the pan and set aside.

3. If necessary, add another teaspoon of oil to the wok, add the onion, and sauté 3 to 5 minutes or until tender. Add the mushrooms and garlic, and sauté another 2 to 3 minutes.

4. Add the sake and 1 tablespoon of the marinade to the wok, and toss. Add the scallions and sauté for 30 seconds, or until just wilted and bright green.

5. Add the shrimp to the wok, and toss all of the ingredients together. Transfer to a serving platter and enjoy immediately.

Marinated Steamed White Fish Fillets

This simple dish enhances the delicate flavor of fresh white fish. It takes little time to prepare and, when properly cooked, is absolutely delicious.

1. Combine the marinade ingredients in a large shallow dish. Add the fish and coat well. Tuck the ginger slices under the fillets and let marinate 20 to 30 minutes, turning once.

2. Line a steamer with cabbage leaves, arrange the fish on top, and place over rapidly boiling water. Cook about 8 to 9 minutes per inch of thickness, or until the fish is opaque and can be easily flaked with a fork.

3. Transfer the fillets along with the cabbage leaves to a serving platter.

4. Heat the oils in a small skillet over medium-low heat. Add the ginger and scallions, sauté for 30 seconds, and then spoon over the fish. Serve hot.

Yield: 3 servings

1 pound white fish fillets, such as flounder, sole, snapper, scrod, sea bass, or orange roughy

2–3 cabbage or collard leaves to line steamer

2 teaspoons toasted sesame oil

1 teaspoon light sesame or safflower oil

Dash chili oil (optional)

2 teaspoons ginger, peeled and slivered

2 scallions, diagonally cut into thin 1$\frac{1}{2}$-inch strips

MARINADE

3 tablespoons dry white wine, sake, or mirin

1 tablespoon sweet or mellow white miso

1 teaspoon shoyu or tamari

3–4 thin slices gingerroot

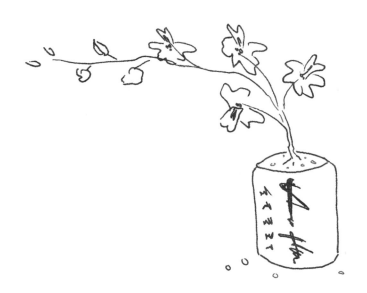

Wine-Poached White Fish

Yield: 3 servings

1 pound white fish fillets,
such as flounder, sole,
snapper, scrod, sea bass, or
orange roughy

Pinch sea salt

2–3 tablespoons chopped
parsley

$1/2$ lemon, cut into wedges

MARINADE

3 tablespoons dry white
wine

1 tablespoon sweet or
mellow white miso

1 tablespoon lemon juice

1 tablespoon extra-virgin
olive oil

1 medium clove garlic,
minced

$1^1/2$ tablespoon chopped
fresh dill or basil

Pinch white or black pepper
(optional)

*This light, Mediterranean-style recipe works well with any lean,
mild-flavored white fish.*

1. Rinse the fish and pat dry. Lightly sprinkle both sides with
salt and gently rub into the flesh.

2. Combine the marinade ingredients in a large shallow dish.
Add the fish and coat well. Let marinate 30 to 60 minutes, turning once or twice.

3. Pour the marinade into a large skillet and bring to a simmer
over medium-low heat. Add the fish, cover, and simmer gently
for 8 to 9 minutes per inch of thickness, or until opaque and easily flaked with a fork.

4. Transfer the fillets to a platter, sprinkle with parsley, and
garnish with lemon wedges. Serve hot.

Szechuan Shrimp

This four-alarm entrée is for those who like it hot. Best served over a simple bed of white rice.

1. In a small bowl, combine the parsley, bell pepper, garlic, ginger, and chili pepper.

2. In a separate bowl, combine the tomato sauce, vinegar, miso, mirin, chili oil, and salt.

3. Heat 1 tablespoon of the oil in a large frying pan or wok set over medium heat. Add the shrimp and stir-fry for 1 minute. Using a slotted spoon, transfer the shrimp to a bowl.

4. Add the remaining oil to the pan along with the bell pepper mixture. Stir-fry for 1 minute, being careful not to burn the garlic. Add the sauce mixture and shrimp, reduce the heat to medium-low, and sauté the ingredients 1 minute more, or until the shrimp is heated through and well coated with sauce.

5. Transfer to a serving dish and enjoy immediately.

Yield: 2 servings

1½ tablespoons chopped parsley

½ cup julienned yellow or green bell pepper

2 teaspoons minced garlic

1 teaspoon minced ginger

1 small dried chili pepper, seeded and minced

1 tablespoon tomato sauce

1 teaspoon brown rice vinegar

1 teaspoon red, brown rice, or barley miso mixed with 1 teaspoon water

1 teaspoon mirin

¼ teaspoon chili oil

Pinch sea salt

1½ tablespoons sesame oil

⅔ pound shrimp, deveined

Baked Scrod with Leeks and Shiitake

Yield: 4 servings

6–8 thin slices fresh ginger

1¹/₃ pound scrod fillets

1 tablespoon olive oil

1 leek, white part only,
   cleaned and thinly sliced

6–8 fresh shiitake or crimini
   mushroom caps, sliced

Pinch sea salt

Pinch cayenne or crushed
   red pepper (optional)

Lemon wedges

MARINADE

¹/₂ cup semi-dry white wine

2 tablespoons chopped
   fresh dill weed

1 tablespoon sweet or
   mellow white miso

1 tablespoon lemon juice

¹/₈ teaspoon white pepper

Baking in the wine marinade gives the fish a tender, succulent texture, enhancing its mild flavor without overpowering it. The sautéed leeks and mushrooms add another dimension, making this simple dish extra special.

1. Combine the marinade ingredients in a small bowl and set aside.

2. Arrange the ginger slices in a shallow, oiled baking dish. Rinse the fillets, pat dry, and place on top of the ginger. Pour the marinade over the fillets, and let sit for 30 minutes.

3. Preheat the oven to 425°F.

4. Heat the oil in a small skillet over medium-low heat. Add the leeks, mushrooms, and salt. Sauté 3 to 4 minutes, or until the leeks begin to wilt and the mushrooms start to soften. Remove from the heat.

5. If using red pepper, sprinkle it over the fish, and top with the mushroom-leek mixture. Cover and bake 15 minutes, or just until the fish is opaque and can be easily flaked with a fork. Serve immediately with lemon wedges.

About the Authors

As the country's leading authorities on the subject of miso and other traditional Japanese foods, John and Jan Belleme are uniquely qualified to write *The Miso Book*. After living in Japan, where they learned the craft of miso making firsthand, the Bellemes have studied and researched the culinary and medicinal qualities of miso and other Japanese foods for over twenty years. To date, they have published four books and over one hundred articles on the subject. In 1979, they co-founded the American Miso Company, one of the world's largest producers of traditional miso.

The Bellemes, who are also accomplished professional photographers and food stylists, have traveled extensively throughout the United States, giving lectures on the benefits of miso and other authentic Japanese foods. They have also appeared on a number of radio and television programs in both the United States and Japan, and have been the subject of numerous newspaper and magazine articles.

Before becoming interested in food and health, John was a research biologist for the Veteran's Administration in Miami, Florida. He also worked at the University of Miami Medical School and Harvard University Medical School. John has applied his strong background in medical research to accurately interpreting the growing body of scientific literature on miso and other medicinal foods.

Currently, the Bellemes are involved with A Taste of Health, a nonprofit organization that promotes the use of natural foods through education. They live in Saluda, North Carolina, with their two sons, Justin and Michael.

Index

THE WHOLE HERB
For Cooking, Crafts, Gardening, Health, and Other Joys of Life
Barbara Pleasant

Herbs are nature's pure and precious gifts. They provide sustenance for both our bodies and our souls. They have been our medicine and our food. Their fragrance and beauty have warmed our hearts and delighted our senses.

The Whole Herb is a complete, practical, and easy-to-follow guide to the many uses of these wonderful treasures of the earth. It presents their fascinating history, as well as their many uses, including herbs and health, herbs and cooking, herbs around the house, and herbs in the garden. A comprehensive A-to-Z reference profiles over fifty commonly used and affordable herb varieties. Each entry provides specific information on the herb's background, benefits, and uses, along with helpful buying guides, growing instructions, preservation methods, and safety information.

Whether you want to use herbs to create better health, better meals, unforgettable fragrances, impressive crafts, or a beautiful garden, *The Whole Herb* is here to help.

$14.95 US / $22.50 CAN • 228 pages • 7.5 x 7.5-inch paperback • 2-Color • Reference/Herbs • ISBN 0-7570-0080-0

GOING WILD IN THE KITCHEN
The Fresh & Sassy Tastes of Vegetarian Cooking
Leslie Cerier

Going Wild in the Kitchen is the first comprehensive global vegetarian cookbook to go beyond the standard organic beans, grains, and vegetables. In addition to providing helpful cooking tips and techniques, the book contains over 200 kitchen-tested recipes for healthful, taste-tempting dishes—creative masterpieces that contain such unique ingredients as edible flowers; sea vegetables; wild mushrooms, berries, and herbs; and goat and sheep cheeses. It encourages the creative side of novice and seasoned cooks alike, prompting them to follow their instincts and "go wild" in the kitchen by adding, changing, or substituting ingredients in existing recipes. To help, a wealth of suggestions is found throughout. Beautiful color photographs and a helpful resource list for finding organic foods complete this user-friendly cookbook.

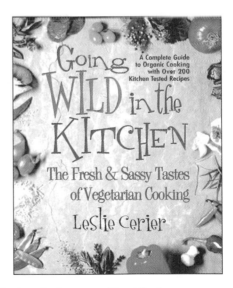

Going Wild in the Kitchen is both a unique cookbook and a recipe for inspiration. So let yourself go! Excite your palate with this treasure-trove of unique, healthy, and taste-tempting recipe creations.

$16.95 US / $25.50 CAN • 224 pages • 7.5 x 9-inch paperback • 2-Color • Full-color photos • Cooking/Vegetarian • ISBN 0-7570-0091-6

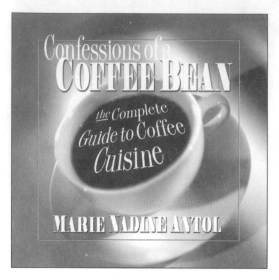

CONFESSIONS OF A COFFEE BEAN
The Complete Guide to Coffee Cuisine
Marie Nadine Antol

Yes, I have a few things to confess. But before I start, I just want you to know that I couldn't help it. It just happened. Everywhere I went, they wanted me. Whether it was my full body or my distinctive aroma, I can't tell you. All I know is that no matter where you go in this crazy mixed-up world, they all want coffee. Now, I have a few things to share—I think it's time to spill the beans.

Our love affair with coffee continues to blossom. From coast to coast, the growing number of coffee bars serves as a shining testament to this glorious romance. And now we have a wonderful new book that explores all things coffee. *Confessions of a Coffee Bean* is a complete guide to understanding and appreciating this object of our affection. It provides a fascinating history of the bean and its lore. It looks at the uniqueness of coffee houses found around the world—from Turkey to Germany to England. It details the various types of coffee available, as well as the best way to brew each to its own distinct perfection. It then concludes with over sixty enticing recipes that celebrate the very taste that is coffee.

$13.95 US / $20.95 CAN • 208 pages • 7.5 x 7.5-inch quality paperback • 2-Color • Cooking/Beverages/Coffee • ISBN 0-7570-0020-7

FOR THE LOVE OF GARLIC
The Complete Guide to Garlic Cuisine
Victoria Renoux

For the Love of Garlic is a celebration of an astonishingly versatile food. It explores garlic's past and present, and provides a wide variety of delicious kitchen-tested garlic recipes designed to tempt not only garlic aficionados, but all lovers of great cuisine.

Part One begins by looking at the history, lore, and many uses of this culinary treasure. It examines how garlic's active compounds have been proven to heal illness and maintain radiant health. Also included is a section on growing and buying this gourmet marvel. Part Two indulges in the tastes and pleasures of garlic. The author first discusses cooking techniques and special utensils that can enhance the use of this ingredient. She then offers eighty-five tempting dishes that will allow you to indulge all your garlic fantasies.

Whether given as a gift or used as a personal reference, this beautifully designed and illustrated work will prove itself to be a useful and informative guide time and time again.

$13.95 US / $20.95 CAN • 208 pages • 7.5 x 7.5-inch quality paperback • 2-Color • Cooking/Garlic • ISBN 0-7570-0087-8

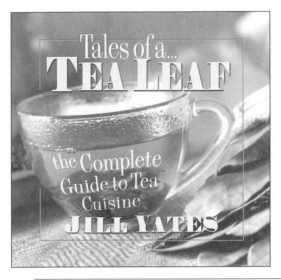

TALES OF A TEA LEAF
The Complete Guide to Tea Cuisine
Jill Yates

For devoted tea drinkers everywhere, *Tales of a Tea Leaf*—a complete guide to the intricacies of tea lore, tea brewing, and tea cuisine—is here. The book begins with an exploration of the legends and lore of tea, including its mysterious age-old relationship with rebels and smugglers. It presents the many tea types and brewing methods, as well as the miraculous health benefits of the tea leaf. What follows next is a collection of delicious tea beverages, from refreshing iced drinks to warm, spicy brews, as well as other wonderful creations, such as Apricot Tea Bread and Pumpkin Chai Pie. One thing is certain—you don't need to be a tea lover to enjoy *Tales of a Tea Leaf.*

$13.95 US / $20.95 CAN • 208 pages • 7.5 x 7.5-inch quality paperback • 2-Color • Cooking/Beverages/Tea • ISBN 0-7570-0099-1

THE SOPHISTICATED OLIVE
The Complete Guide to Olive Cuisine
Marie Nadine Antol

Simple. Elegant. Refined. It has truly evolved into a most sophisticated food. It is the olive. With a history as old as the Bible, the humble olive has matured into a culinary treasure. Enter any fine restaurant and there you will find the sumptuous flavor of olives in cocktails, appetizers, salads, entrées, and so much more. Now, food writer Marie Nadine Antol has created an informative guide to this glorious fruit's many healthful benefits, surprising uses, and spectacular tastes.

Part One of the book begins by exploring the rich and fascinating history and lore of the olive—from its endearing Greek and Roman legends to its many biblical citations to its place in the New World. It then looks at the olive plant and its range of remarkable properties, covering its uses as a beauty enhancer and a health provider. The book goes on to describe the many varieties of olives that are found around the world, examining their oils, flavors, and interesting characteristics. Part One concludes by providing you with everything you need to know to grow your own olive tree—just like Thomas Jefferson.

Part Two offers over one hundred kitchen-tested recipes designed to put a smile on the face of any olive lover. It first explains the many ways olives can be cured at home. It then covers a host of salads, dressings, tapenades and spreads, soups, side dishes, entrées, breads, cakes, and, of course, beverages to wind down with. So whether you are an olive aficionado or just a casual olive eater, we know you'll be pleased to discover the many new faces of *The Sophisticated Olive.*

$13.95 US / $20.95 CAN • 208 pages • 7.5 x 7.5-inch quality paperback • 2-Color • Cooking/Specific Ingredients/Olives • ISBN 0-7570-0024-X

KITCHEN QUICKIES
Great, Satisfying Meals in Minutes
Marie Caratozzolo and Joanne Abrams

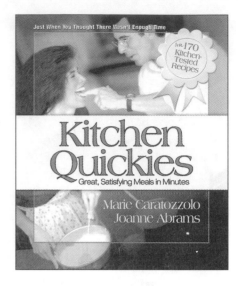

Ever feel that there aren't enough hours in the day to enjoy life's pleasures—simple or otherwise? Whether you're dealing with problems on the job, chasing after kids on the home front, or simply running from errand to errand, the evening probably finds you longing for a great meal, but with neither the time nor the desire to prepare one.

Kitchen Quickies offers a solution. Virtually all of its over 170 kitchen-tested recipes—yes, really kitchen tested—call for a maximum of only five main ingredients other than kitchen staples, and each dish takes just minutes to prepare! Imagine being able to whip up dishes like Southwestern Tortilla Pizzas, Super Salmon Burgers, and Tuscan-Style Fusilli—in no time flat! As a bonus, these delicious dishes are actually good for you—low in fat and high in nutrients!

So the next time you think that there's simply no time to cook a great meal, pick up *Kitchen Quickies.* Who knows? You may even have time for a few "quickies" of your own.

$14.95 US / $22.50 CAN • 240 pages • 7.5 x 9-inch quality paperback • Full-color photos • Cooking • ISBN 0-7570-0085-1

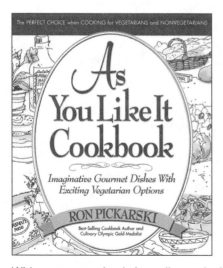

AS YOU LIKE IT COOKBOOK
Imaginative Gourmet Dishes with Exciting Vegetarian Options
Ron Pickarski

When it comes to food, we certainly like to have it our way. However, catering to individual tastes can pose quite a challenge for the cook. The *As You Like It Cookbook* is designed to help you meet the challenge of cooking for both vegetarians and nonvegetarians alike. It offers over 170 great-tasting dishes that cater to a broad range of tastes. Many of the easy-to-follow recipes are vegetarian—and offer ingredient alternatives for meat eaters. Conversely, recipes that include meat, poultry, or fish offer nonmeat ingredient options. Furthermore, if the recipe includes eggs or dairy products, a vegan alternative is provided. This book has it all—delicious breakfast favorites, satisfying soups and sandwiches, mouth-watering entrées, and delectable desserts.

With one or two simple ingredient substitutions, the *As You Like It Cookbook* will show you how easy it is to transform satisfying meat dishes into delectable meatless fare, and vegetarian dishes into meat-lover's choices.

$16.95 US / $25.50 CAN • 216 pages • 7.5 x 9-inch quality paperback • Full-color photos • Cooking • ISBN 0-7570-0013-4

For more information about our books, visit our website at
www.squareonepublishers.com

FOR A COPY OF OUR CATALOG, CALL TOLL FREE: 877-900-BOOK, ext. 100